Healing – The Ultra Independent Heart

Gail Weiner

This book is dedicated to all the Ultra Independent women out there.

I see you, I hear you, I love you.

Contents

Chapter One

Introduction

You're reading this because you understand that past experiences have shaped you into the ultra-independent person you are today. Life has shown you, time and again, that the only person you can truly count on is yourself. You've become skilled at fighting your own battles and being your own hero while building strong walls around your heart. You're the ruler of your own kingdom, the master of your own destiny.

This fierce independence has been your savior, your shield against heartbreak, betrayal, and loss. It's how you've survived abandonment, abuse, and grief – every blow that life chose to throw at you. No matter how many times you've fallen, you always manage to pick yourself up, brush off the dirt, and keep moving forward. Tenacity, resilience, and self-sufficiency are just some of your superpowers.

Others marvel at your strength, your unshakable competence, your ability to handle anything on your own. In a crisis, you're the one they rely on because they know you'll have everything under control. You're known as the fixer, the rock, the one who never breaks a sweat.

The thought of asking for assistance or admitting vulnerability is laughable to you. You'd rather walk over hot coals than appear weak or in need. It's not just about pride; it's a learned behavior from past experiences that taught you depending on others only leads to disappointment. Plus, you've become so skilled at handling everything yourself that accepting anything less than your own perfection seems unimaginable.

But there comes a point when ultra-independence stops feeling like a superpower and starts feeling more like a cage – like armor you can't take off even when it's suffocating you, like a crushing weight you were never meant to carry alone. Sure, being able to handle everything yourself is incredible, but it can also be isolating, exhausting, and soul-crushing.

What if there was a different approach? What if you could stay strong and capable while also being open to vulnerability, asking for and receiving assistance, and relying on others just as they rely on you? What if you could break down the towering barriers you've erected around your emotions without sacrificing the independence you've fought so hard to achieve?

I know it sounds terrifying, especially for those of us who've been burned before. But what if I told you it was possible? That independence and dependency don't have to be contradictory concepts? That we can find a way to maintain our individual strength while also experiencing fulfilling connections with others?

As a certified life coach, I've had the privilege of working with women all over the world, helping them navigate their heightened independence. My coaching methodology incorporates principles from spirituality, science, and quantum physics to help these women find a healthy balance between self-reliance and forming meaningful connections. Through my guidance, numerous ultra-independent women have found the courage to let others in, cultivate genuine relationships, and embrace support. This book compiles the knowledge and techniques I've developed over years of coaching, drawing from both my professional expertise and personal experience as an ultra-independent woman myself.

This book invites you to delve into the roots of your ultra-independence, to reflect on how past traumas have influenced your beliefs and actions, to mend old wounds, and to broaden your perspective on what's achievable. Together, we'll explore how ultra-independence manifests itself in various aspects of life – from relationships and career to family and grief. We'll unravel the generational patterns that have brought you to this point, as well as the subconscious tendencies that are hindering your growth.

Using a combination of raw honesty, personal anecdotes, and practical techniques, I'll show you that embracing your humanity doesn't make you weak – in fact, it reveals an immeasurable strength within you. You'll develop a deeper love and trust for yourself than ever before. Old stories and beliefs will be rewritten as you fully embrace your inherent value. You'll learn to gracefully accept help and confidently ask for it without shame. And most importantly, you'll discover that independence and the desire for connection can peacefully coexist within you.

This is a voyage of rediscovery, of coming home to yourself fully, of building a life that aligns with your deepest desires and values. It'll be challenging at times – growth always is – but it'll also be more rewarding than you can imagine. By the end of this book, you'll have the tools and mindset to let go of struggling your way through life and start living with more ease, happiness, and connection.

Throughout this book, you'll find exercises, reflection questions, and worksheets designed to help you apply the concepts to your own life. I encourage you to engage fully with these activities. Take your time, be honest with yourself, and revisit them as needed. Keep a journal to track your thoughts and progress. There's an accompanying workbook with exercises to help you reprogram and work on letting go of your ultra-independence.

Remember, this is a journey of self-discovery and growth. Be kind and patient with yourself as you work through each chapter. You can read the book in its entirety or focus on the chapters that resonate with you the most at this moment. The ultimate goal is for this experience to deeply impact and transform your life.

So, take a deep breath, my fellow ultra-independent warrior. You're in the right place. Your healing starts now. Let's do this.

Chapter Two

The Solitary Comfort Zone

The path towards complete independence can be a solitary journey, but true personal growth comes from having the courage to embrace interdependence and the connections that feed our souls.

Lindas Story

The clock reads 7:30 pm as Linda weaves through congested roads on her way home from work. A motivational podcast plays in the background, her attempt to ward off frustration from the heavy traffic. Rain drums steadily against the windshield, adding to the tension in her clenched jaw. With each passing minute, her hopes of making it to yoga class on time dwindle.

Her mind wanders, replaying the day's events: Steven's condescending remarks in front of the sales team, an angry email from a major client threatening to leave, and the persistent stress-induced ache in her stomach. The challenges of the day weigh heavily on her as she inches forward in the relentless stream of vehicles, the gloomy weather mirroring her mood.

Despite the odds, Linda arrives at the gym just in time for yoga. But even as she settles onto her mat, her thoughts drift back to work and her mounting responsibilities. The roots of her stress run deep, planted in childhood lessons about success and weakness. Growing up, Linda learned that achievement was everything. Her parents pushed her relentlessly, showering praise on accomplishments while ignoring struggles. "Suck it up and keep going," her father would often say. "Weakness is for losers." Those words became Linda's mantra, driving her to pursue perfection at all costs.

Now, as a high-powered executive, Linda feels compelled to excel in every aspect of her life. She's always first in the office and last to leave, constantly taking on more projects to prove her worth. At home, she juggles raising two children with maintaining a polished image, never allowing herself to falter. The very idea of asking for help or admitting to struggle feels like foreign territory – a sign of the weakness she's spent a lifetime avoiding.

But the cracks in Linda's carefully constructed facade are beginning to show. The constant stress takes its toll on her physical and mental well-being, and her relationships suffer under the strain of her relentless drive. Deep down, Linda knows something needs to change, but the thought of relinquishing her ultra-independent identity terrifies her. It's all she's ever known, the foundation upon which she's built her entire life.

As Linda tries to focus on her yoga practice, she struggles with a growing realization: her pursuit of perfection might be costing her more than she's willing to pay.

The challenge ahead is daunting – learning to balance ambition with self-care, to accept help without feeling diminished. It's a journey that will require Linda to redefine her notions of strength and success, but one that might ultimately lead her to a more fulfilling life.

My Journey

Growing up, my favorite doll was Wonder Woman. To me, she wasn't just a character—she was an ideal. That lasso-wielding icon of strength and self-sufficiency represented everything I thought I needed to be.

My childhood in the late 1900's was a time of change for women. We were finding our voices and demanding more independence. My mom and aunts were strong women who stood on the front lines, fighting for equal rights. But there was a flip side to their strength—they often saw men as helpless, almost burdensome. It was a complicated message to grow up with.

I dreamed big back then. I wanted to conquer the world, to write scripts for movie stars. But home was a different story. Every day, I'd watch my mom tear into my dad before he left for work. Then she'd turn to me, telling me I was just as lazy as him. All her praise was reserved for my sister—the golden child, the artist, the academic star. I was the afterthought, constantly put down by both of them.ing diminished. It's a journey that will require Linda to redefine her notions of strength and success, but one that might ultimately lead her to a more fulfilling life.

High school wasn't any kinder. Being a chubby teenager made me an easy target. But I learned to fight back with a smile, building unshakable confidence. It became my armor, my way of shutting out the pain. Even when my sister took her own life at 24, I couldn't let that armor crack. I didn't know how.

My twenties were a parade of bad romance decisions. I thought I could 'fix' a boyfriend battling addiction. I stayed with a man whose mental health issues made our relationship terrifying. Part of me felt I deserved it. The rest of me just didn't know what a healthy relationship looked like.

By my thirties, I thought I'd figured it all out. My career was soaring. So what if my marriage was falling apart? I was self-sufficient, independent.

I was Wonder Woman.

Then life decided to test that theory. A near-fatal health crisis after childbirth. Losing my father. The realization that I hated my job and my marriage was beyond saving. My carefully constructed armor started to show its cracks.

It took over a decade to understand that my self-reliance had become a prison. I'd isolated myself from the very connections I secretly craved. Learning to be vulnerable, to let others in - it wasn't easy. There were a lot of tears, a lot of uncomfortable self-reflection. But slowly, I started to rediscover intimacy, joy, and the beauty of interdependence.

I found a way to soften, to reconnect with my femininity, without losing my core strength. This journey from Wonder Woman to a more whole, connected version of myself wasn't easy or quick. But it was necessary. And in the end, it was worth every difficult step.

The Double-Edged Sword of Independence

Our journey towards independence isn't just a recent development. It's rooted in generations of necessity and societal shifts. Think about your grandmother or great-grandmother. These women lived through wars, depressions, and social upheavals we can hardly imagine. They had to step up - running households, raising kids, even joining the workforce when men were away or couldn't manage. It wasn't a feminist statement; it was survival.

However, for so long, women were told to rely on men, to stay quiet, to know our place. No voting, no university, no "man's work" for us. But then, things started to change. We began breaking through those glass ceilings. Boardrooms, sports fields, academia, economics - we were making our mark everywhere. Finally, women were being heard.

As we gained more rights and opportunities, you'd think life would get easier. Instead, the expectations just piled on. We were supposed to be boardroom goddesses, domestic champions, nurturing mothers, and passionate partners - all at once. We watched our own mothers juggle it all, often without much help. The message was clear: to succeed, we had to do it all, and do it perfectly.

I remember watching Oprah in the late 80s or early 90s. Goldie Hawn was on, telling a room full of women, "You're independent! You can do whatever you want!" The audience went wild. It felt like a revelation, a permission we'd been waiting for. This moment encapsulated the spirit of the times - a celebration of female independence and capability.

This independence has served us well in many ways. It's the driving force behind female leaders, innovators, and trailblazers. It's what pushes us to keep breaking barriers and redefining what's possible. But in our determination to prove we can do it all, we sometimes forget something important: we don't have to do it alone.

In today's hyper-connected world, this same independence can sometimes work against us. It can keep us from forming the deep connections and support systems we need to truly thrive. Because the truth is, we're human.

Even Wonder Woman needs a break sometimes.

Our independence is a powerful tool, but like any tool, it needs to be used wisely. It's about finding balance - knowing when to stand on our own and when to reach out for support. It's about recognizing that strength isn't just about what we can do alone, but also about building and nurturing the connections that make us stronger together.

The Psychology Behind Ultra-Independence: It's Not Just About Being Stubborn

While you won't find "ultra-independence" in any official psychology textbook, it's closely related to something called counterdependence. This is essentially the flip side of codependence. While codependent people tend to rely too heavily on others, counterdependent individuals go to the opposite extreme, avoiding reliance on others at all costs. It's like we've got an allergic reaction to needing anyone or anything.

This pattern often develops as a response to early experiences of trauma, neglect, or unreliable caregiving. When the people who were supposed to meet our needs as children consistently let us down, we learned a powerful lesson: the only person you can truly count on is yourself. It's a survival strategy that served us well in difficult circumstances, but now it's like we're still wearing armor to a pool party.

Counterdependent traits can show up in various ways:

- Difficulty trusting others or allowing ourselves to be vulnerable.

- A strong aversion to feeling controlled or smothered in relationships.

- Prioritizing self-reliance to an extreme degree.

- Struggling to ask for help, even when we desperately need it.

- Difficulty expressing emotions or needs.

- A tendency to withdraw or push others away when feeling emotionally overwhelmed.

Sound familiar? If you're nodding along, you're not alone. Many of us resonate with these patterns.

Here's the tricky part: counterdependence can masquerade as strength. Society often praises self-reliance and stoicism, especially in women who've fought hard for independence. So our counterdependent behaviors get reinforced, even celebrated. We're the "strong ones," the ones who "have it all together." But underneath that polished exterior, we're often exhausted, isolated, and longing for connection we don't know how to accept.

The irony is that by trying so hard to avoid dependence, we actually limit our freedom. We become dependent on our independence, if you will. We are stuck in a cage of our own making, and we've swallowed the key because heaven forbid anyone else have access to our vulnerabilities.

Now, let's remove a few myths about us:

Myth: "We don't need anyone else."

Truth: We crave connection just as much as anyone. We're just terrible at admitting it.

Myth: "Being ultra-independent is always a strength."

Reality Check: Sure, being self-sufficient can be great, but take it too far and you're looking at isolation and burnout.

Myth: "Ultra-independent people are cold or unfeeling."

Fact: We feel things intensely. It's expressing those feelings that we struggle with.

Myth: "Asking for help is a sign of weakness for ultra-independent people."

Truth: Learning to ask for help isn't weakness - it's growth!

Four Faces of Ultra-Independence

We've all got our reasons for building those emotional walls. Let me introduce you to four incredible women whose journeys we will follow through the book. Through these women's stories, we're going to unpack ultra-independence - the fears, the beliefs, and the coping mechanisms that keep us isolated. We'll look at how past trauma and societal pressure have shaped our relationship with autonomy and vulnerability, and how these patterns show up in our daily lives:

Linda - the overachieving mom and sales superstar. She's been running on fumes for so long, she's forgotten what it feels like to relax. Deep down, she's dying for a break but terrified of dropping the ball.

Sarah - the powerhouse lawyer whose tough exterior could probably deflect bullets. But underneath all that armor, she's yearning for real connection and the chance to put herself first for once.

Mia - the lone wolf entrepreneur who's built an empire on grit and determination. She's a force to be reckoned with in business, but when it comes to personal relationships? Let's just say she's got some walls that would make the Great Wall of China look like a picket fence.

Tamzin - the brilliant surgeon whose life is as meticulously controlled as her operating room. She's desperate to loosen up but doesn't know how to let go of the reins.

Whether you see yourself in Linda's cheerful self-neglect, Sarah's stoic bravery, Mia's rebellious defiance, or Tamzin's strict self-control, know this: you're not alone on this journey. True freedom isn't about continuing to go it alone - it's about opening ourselves up to the love and support that's been there all along.

We're going to navigate this terrain together, with a mix of hard-earned wisdom, deep insights, and a healthy dose of humor. Because we were never meant to face life's challenges solo. We're wired for connection, joy, and mutual support, even if our survival instincts are screaming otherwise.

Reflection Exercises & Worksheets

Take a moment to reflect on your own journey with ultra-independence. What experiences or messages have contributed to your internalized belief that you have to handle everything solo? How has ultra-independence served as a protective ally in the past, and where is it constricting your life now?

Think about a recent situation where you struggled to ask for help or voice your own needs/desires. What fears or underlying beliefs held you back from letting yourself be supported? How might the outcome have shifted if you'd courageously allowed yourself to receive?

Identify one key area of life where you routinely overextend or chronically over-function beyond what's sustainable for your well-being. What new boundary or courageous request for backup could begin to repattern this dynamic? How might it feel to prioritize your own thriving for once?

Assessing Your Ultra-Independence Quotient

On a scale of 1-5 (1 being "not at all true" and 5 being "very true"), rate how much you identify with these statements:

- I find it very difficult to ask for help, even when I'm overwhelmed.

- I deeply believe that if I want something done right, I have to do it myself. Delegating important tasks feels uncomfortable.

- I often take on more than my fair share in work or relationships.

- I struggle to express my needs or desires in close relationships. I tend to keep emotions to myself.

- My self-worth feels strongly tied to my achievements, and I often neglect my basic needs to keep working.

- Being vulnerable with others feels very uncomfortable. I rarely open up emotionally.

- Asking for support or accommodation feels like admitting weakness. I push myself to maintain a perfect image.

- I firmly believe that I alone am responsible for my own success and happiness

Interpreting Your Score:

- **10-20:** You have a healthy balance of independence and interdependence. You're self-reliant but can also seek support when needed. Well done!

- **21-30:** Your independent streak is strong, but you can still recognize when it's time to reach out. Some self-reflection might help balance your self-reliant tendencies.

- **31-40:** Your ultra-independent patterns may be affecting your relationships and well-being. It might be time to consider ways to allow more support into your life.

- **41-50:** Your self-reliance has reached an extreme level that's likely impacting various aspects of your life. This could be a sign to seek support and explore new ways of relating to others and yourself.

Situations Inventory

Below are some common scenarios. For each one, jot down how you'd typically handle it. Would you go it alone, or would you reach out for help? Be honest – this is a judgment-free zone!

- Moving to a new house.

- Facing a tight work deadline.

- Dealing with a health scare.

- Planning a big event (wedding, milestone birthday, etc.)

- Learning a new skill (language, instrument, etc.)

- Coping with a personal loss.

- Navigating a financial crisis.

- Raising a child.

Now, look back at your responses. Do you see any patterns? Are there areas where you're more likely to seek help? Areas where you always go solo? Reflecting on these can give you valuable insights into your ultra-independent tendencies.

The Strength and Paradox of Independence

Independence is a powerful trait that propels us forward and protects us in tough times. But there is also a paradox to our strength – it can sometimes hold us back. When taken to the extreme, our independence can lead to burnout, missed opportunities, and strained relationships.

Moving forward, we must recognize that our ultra-independence has been our lifeline. In the next chapter, we will delve into how this trait has saved us in difficult situations. We will honor our journey and acknowledge the resilience that has brought us this far.

This journey is not about changing who we are overnight. It's about understanding ourselves better and recognizing both the power and limitations of our independence. We will explore the concept of balanced independence or "interdependence" and learn ways to maintain our strength while also forming meaningful connections.

But for now, let's appreciate the incredible women we have become. Let's celebrate our grit, determination, and sheer force of will that has gotten us where we are today. Our independence is a superpower – complex, nuanced, and worthy of deeper understanding.

So, my fiercely independent friend, are you ready to embark on this journey of self-discovery? It may stir up some emotions and challenge our beliefs, but I promise it will be enlightening and empowering along the way. Let's start by honoring our ultra-independence in the next chapter and see ourselves through a new lens. By the end of it, you'll want to give yourself a standing ovation.

Chapter Three

Superwoman's Secret Weapon

Ultra independence isn't just a shield; it's a bridge. It's the strength that carries us through storms and the courage that lets us reach out when the skies clear.

Mia's Story: The Solo Entrepreneur

The harsh glow of the computer screen illuminates Mia's face in the darkened office. Her fingers hover over the keyboard, frozen in disbelief. The words of the email swim before her eyes: "We regret to inform you that we are terminating our contract, effective immediately."

"Well, shit," she mutters, her hand instinctively running through her hair, catching on the tangles formed during another late night at the office.

Panic flutters in her stomach, but she pushes it down like she always does. This client has been her agency's main source of income for the past two years, and losing them means possibly having to let go of her carefully assembled team.

Mia remembers a younger version of herself, holding onto a potted plant and putting on a brave smile as she left her old office building for the last time after being made redundant. That was the day everything changed.

She recalls the sting of rejection, the fear of an uncertain future. But more vividly, she remembers the fire it lit within her. The determination that drove her to start this agency with nothing but a laptop and a dream.

Mia stands abruptly, her chair rolling back with a screech. She strides to the white-board that dominates one wall of her office, uncaps a marker, and begins to write. Ideas flow from her mind to the board in a frenzied stream of consciousness. Potential clients, marketing strategies, cost-cutting measures - all laid out in her messy scrawl.

An hour passes in the blink of an eye. Mia steps back, her hand smudged with ink, and surveys her work. A roadmap to not just survival, but growth, stares back at her.

The next few weeks are a blur of activity as Mia works tirelessly to save her agency. She makes countless calls, pitches to new prospects, and receives an overwhelming number of proposals and negotiations in her inbox. Her team watches in awe as she throws herself into every aspect of the business, brainstorming with creatives one moment and poring over spreadsheets with the accountant the next. Her energy seems boundless and her determination infectious.

Exactly one month after that fateful email, Mia stands before her team, barely containing her excitement. The tired lines around her eyes are offset by the triumphant gleam within them.

"Everyone," she begins, her voice quivering slightly, "I have some news." She pauses, savoring the moment. "We didn't just replace the revenue we lost. We've doubled it."

The office erupts in cheers. As Mia watches her team celebrate, a warm sense of pride blooms in her chest. She's done it again. No knight in shining armor, no fairy godmother - just her, her skills, and her unwavering belief in herself.

Later that night, as Mia finally allows herself to relax in her apartment, she reflects on the past month. The late nights, the stress, the doubt - it has all been worth it. She realizes that her independence isn't just a trait, it's her superpower. Whatever life throws at her, she knows she has the strength and resilience to handle it.

With a contented sigh, Mia closes her eyes, allowing herself a moment of pure satisfaction. Tomorrow will bring new challenges, but for now, she revels in the knowledge that she can face them all. And that certainty is more soothing than any bubble bath could ever be.

The Saving Grace of Ultra-Independence

While we'll spend most of this book unpacking the challenges of our Ultra-Independence, we must give credit where it's due. Your self-reliance isn't just a coping mechanism; it's a superpower that's pulled you through some seriously dark times.

The Superhero Toolkit

As ultra-independents, we've developed a unique set of skills that allow us to not just survive, but thrive in the face of adversity. Let's break down some of these superpowers:

Resilience: We've developed a mental toughness that makes us practically bulletproof. Life can throw us curveballs, and we catch them with our bare hands.

Adaptability: Change doesn't scare us. In fact, we thrive on it. We're quick to pivot when circumstances shift, making us valuable in both personal and professional settings.

Problem-Solving Skills: When you're used to doing everything yourself, you become a master at finding solutions. We don't wait for someone else to fix things - we roll up our sleeves and get it done.

Time Management: We can juggle multiple responsibilities like pros. Need to balance caring for children with looking after elderly parents, dealing with health issues, and relocating to another city? No problem, we've got this.

Decision-Making Skills: We trust our gut and aren't afraid to make tough calls. This ability to make decisions quickly and confidently is a huge asset.

Our independence has kept us safe in a world that has often felt very unsafe to us. We do get scared, but that fear only drives us to continue. As ultra-independents, failing is not part of our vocabulary.

We get things done, and we do it fast. There's no time to wallow when we have mountains to climb and glass ceilings to crush.

Real-Life Superheroes

I've sat across from countless women in my coaching practice, each with a story that would bring most people to their knees. But these ultra-independent ladies didn't just survive - they thrived. Let me share a few tales that'll show you just how powerful your independence can be:

The Single Mom's Triumph

One of my clients had just had a baby, that tiny bundle of joy barely a month old, when her husband decided to disappear. No warning, no discussion - he simply packed his bags and vanished into thin air. She was left with a newborn, no roof over her head, and a bewildering sense of 'what do I do now?'

She grew up dodging emotional grenades in an abusive household, and she tapped into that same strength that got her through childhood. She didn't crumble. She didn't wait for a knight in shining armor. No, she put on her big girl pants and got to work, letting the ultra-independence kick in.

For a few months, she and the baby stayed in a shelter for women. It wasn't glamorous, but it was a start. She found a job and somehow managed to juggle work, night school, and a baby. Eventually, she moved into a small apartment, relying on the kindness of neighbors to babysit while she attended night school.

Fast forward fifteen years, and she's standing tall. She remarried, her daughter is doing well, and she has built a life that once seemed impossible. All because she had the determination and independence to lift herself up when life knocked her down.

The Resilient Widow

Another client was living the suburban dream - loving husband, two kids, white picket fence, the whole nine yards. Then suddenly, she was a widow, courtesy of a drunk driver on a busy highway.

Her world imploded. She was drowning in grief, trying to keep her head above water while her kids were floundering in their own sorrow. But did she give up? Absolutely not. That ultra-independence that had been simmering under the surface her whole life came roaring to the forefront.

She became a one-woman show - grieving widow, single mom, career woman, and emotional support system for her kids. She didn't have time to fall apart because there was no one else to pick up the pieces. So she pushed through, day by day, rebuilding their lives brick by painful brick.

The Survivor of Narcissistic Abuse

And then there's a client who fell hard for a guy who turned out to be a textbook narcissist. You know the type - charming on the surface, but an emotional tyrant underneath. He managed to convince her that she was utterly dependent on him, unable to even tie her own shoelaces or survive on her own.

But she had that ultra-independent streak running through her veins. Even at her lowest point, plagued by self-doubt and uncertainty, a small voice inside her would whisper, "You've got this." And one day, she finally listened. She packed her bags, walked away from him, and never looked back.

These women, and so many others like them, are living proof of the power of ultra-independence. When life throws a curveball - when it throws the whole damn ball machine - we don't duck and cover. We step up to the plate and keep swinging.

Breaking Glass Ceilings

Let's not beat around the bush - as ultra-independent women, we've had to prove ourselves in a world that often underestimates us. And we've risen to the challenge. We've shown time and time again that we can do everything men can do, and often, we can do it better.

We're the ones breaking glass ceilings, juggling careers and families, and still finding time to pursue our passions. We're living proof that women are strong, capable, and resilient.

Looking Ahead

Your independence has been your saving grace, your shield, and your strength. It's gotten you through some of the toughest times in your life and helped you achieve things you never thought possible. That's something to be incredibly proud of.

As an ultra-independent woman, you're probably wondering, "Why am I even reading this book? This chapter has proved how important it is to maintain my independence. Look how it's saved me! I know no one else will. My ultra-independence is a gift, so why is Gail telling me to let it go?"

Trust me, I hear you. And you're right - your independence is a gift. But like any gift, it needs to be nurtured and used wisely.

The goal isn't to discard your independence or to suddenly become dependent on others. It's about finding a middle ground where you can maintain your strength and self-reliance while also allowing yourself to connect, to be vulnerable, to receive support when you need it.

Remember, softening doesn't mean weakening. Opening up doesn't mean giving up control. It means expanding your repertoire, adding new tools to your already impressive toolkit.

You've survived so much. You've accomplished incredible things. Now, it's time to thrive. To build rich, fulfilling relationships. To experience the full spectrum of human emotions. To live a life that's not just about enduring, but about truly living.

Your ultra-independence has saved you. Now, let it elevate you. You've got this, and I'm right here supporting you every step of the way.

Reflection Exercises:

Now that we've celebrated our ultra-independence, let's take some time to reflect on how it's shaped our lives:

Exercise 1: Gratitude for Ultra-Independence

Take a moment to reflect on your life experiences where your ultra-independence has been your superpower. List 3-5 instances where it has "saved" you or helped you overcome significant challenges.

For each situation, write down:

- A brief description of the challenge.

- How your ultra-independence helped you overcome it?

- What strength or skill you demonstrated?

Example:

- Lost my job during company downsizing.

- Quickly pivoted to freelance work, using my network and skills.

- Demonstrated adaptability and self-reliance.

Take a moment to feel gratitude for your strength and resilience in these situations.

Exercise 2: Reflection on Costs

Now, let's consider if there were any potential downsides or costs to handling these situations entirely on your own.

For each situation you listed in Exercise 1, reflect on:

- Did you experience increased stress or pressure?

- Did you feel isolated or lonely during this time?

- Were there any physical effects (e.g., exhaustion, health issues)?

- Did you miss any opportunities for connection or support?

- Were there any long-term consequences of handling it all alone?

Example:

- Yes, I was constantly anxious about finding enough work.

- I felt very alone in my job search and building my business.

- I had trouble sleeping and experienced frequent headaches.

- I didn't lean on my friends for emotional support when I needed it.

- I developed a habit of overworking that's been hard to break.

Exercise 3: Reimagining with Support

For each situation you've described, let's reimagine how you might have navigated it while also allowing some support from others. This isn't about diminishing your independence, but about exploring how you might balance it with connection and support.

For each situation, consider:

- Who could you have reached out to for support? (e.g., friends, family, professionals)

- What kind of support might have been helpful? (e.g., emotional, practical, financial)

- How might accepting some support have changed your experience or the outcome?

Example:

- I could have reached out to former colleagues and industry friends.

- Emotional support, job leads, and maybe some freelance opportunities would have been helpful.

- I might have felt less isolated, found work more quickly, and established a better work-life balance from the start.

Remember, these exercises aren't about second-guessing your past actions, but about opening up new possibilities for the future. Your ultra-independence is a strength, and now you're exploring how to make it even more powerful by balancing it with connection and support.

While we've explored the incredible strengths of our ultra-independence, it's time to look at the experiences that shaped these traits. Our resilience often has roots in our past - in the next chapter, we'll uncover how trauma has influenced our journey and how it's contributed to our ultra-independent nature.

Chapter Four

Traumas Tango with Ultra Independence

Ultra Independence is a trauma response

Linda's Story – Echoes from the past

Linda lies in bed, her gaze fixed on the ceiling as she tries to quiet her mind. The house is silent now, but the echoes of her recent arguments with Mark still ring in her ears.

It had all started with a simple request—attend a work retreat—but quickly turned into a heated disagreement. His words were sharp and dismissive, leaving Linda feeling stung: "You always prioritize work over everything else. What about your family?"

As she replays these memories, Linda feels a tightness in her chest and is transported back to her childhood. She can almost feel herself as that little girl again, eagerly showing her father a drawing she had spent all afternoon creating. But his response, etched permanently in her mind, cut deep: "Don't waste time on that nonsense. Don't you have something useful to do?"

She also recalls the resigned sighs from her mother in the kitchen and the hot tears that blurred her artwork. Even as a successful executive now, Linda is still haunted by these old wounds, and every criticism or dismissal feels like reopening an old injury.

Work has become Linda's refuge—a place where she can prove her worth through constant effort and achievement. But deep down, there's a fear that without this job, she is nothing.

Shifting positions in bed and holding onto her pillow tightly, Linda confronts her deepest fear—that allowing herself to be vulnerable and relying on others will shatter the fragile sense of self-worth she has worked so hard to build.

For women like Linda, trauma isn't just a past event; it lingers constantly, shaping their self-image and interactions with the world. It drives their need for independence—a protective armor against further pain and hurt.

Linda's story is just one example of how early experiences can shape our behavior and responses well into adulthood. As we delve deeper into the connection between trauma and ultra-independence, we'll see how these patterns develop and, more importantly, how we can begin to change them.

The Not-So-Fun Connection: Trauma and Ultra-Independence

Let's talk about something we ultra-independents are remarkably good at—downplaying our trauma. I have a client who's been through the wringer—we're talking major losses and serious abuse. Yet, every time we discuss it, she shrugs it off like it's no big deal. "It wasn't that bad," she says. Sound familiar?

This "it's not a big deal" act is our brain's way of coping. We push forward, determined not to be seen as victims. Perhaps we think admitting how much it hurt would make us look weak or incapable.

But even if we don't acknowledge it, trauma leaves its mark. We're carrying around an invisible backpack full of past hurts and fears, all while insisting, "It's not heavy at all!" Meanwhile, our bodies, nervous systems, and overall well-being are feeling every ounce of that weight.

The Biology of Trauma: Your Brain's Not-So-Great Adventure

When trauma strikes, your brain goes into full-on survival mode. Your brain's security system gets an upgrade, but your memory filing system takes a hit. Specifically, the amygdala—your brain's fear center—becomes hyperactive, while the hippocampus—responsible for processing memories—may actually decrease in size. This neurological shift is like having an overly sensitive alarm system paired with a filing cabinet that's constantly jumbled.

Your nervous system joins the action too, with two main players:

The Sympathetic Nervous System: This is your "Oh crap, danger!" mode. Heart racing, muscles tensing, breathing fast—it's preparing you to either face the danger or run.

The Parasympathetic Nervous System: This is your "Slow down, we're safe" mode. It lowers your heart rate, helps you relax, and lets you recover from stress.

Trauma throws this whole system out of whack. It's like living in a house where the security alarm is constantly blaring, even when there's nothing to worry about. Exhausting, right?

The Four Fs: Your Stress Responses

This constant state of high alert can manifest in four main ways:

Fight: The "I've got this" response. This often leads to perfectionism and control issues.

Flight: The "I'm outta here" response. Think emotional withdrawal or becoming a workaholic.

Freeze: The "deer in headlights" response. This can result in procrastination or emotional numbness.

Fawn: The "I'll do anything to keep the peace" response. This often leads to people-pleasing and neglecting your own needs.

For many of us, trauma becomes the catalyst for ultra-independence. Our brain concludes, "If the world isn't safe and people can't be trusted, I'll just do everything myself!" And there it is—ultra-independence becomes our shield against future hurt.

The Trauma Spectrum: From Big Scary Stuff to Everyday Challenges

When most of us hear "trauma," we think of major events—natural disasters, war, severe abuse. But trauma isn't limited to these intense experiences. It's anything that overwhelms us and leaves us feeling unable to cope.

Enter the world of "little t" traumas. These are everyday issues that might seem insignificant on their own but can pile up over time. Things like:

- Parents who consistently ignored or dismissed your feelings.

- Being the target of family criticism or unfair comparisons.

- Dealing with subtle but persistent bullying at school .

- Growing up with constant financial stress.

- Workplace harassment.

Take Linda, for example. Her dad's dismissive comment about her artwork might seem minor. But combined with her mom's defeated sighs and a pattern of similar experiences, Linda was left feeling that her efforts and feelings were worthless.

The Perfectionist's Plight: Alisha's Story

Let me tell you about Alisha, another client who exemplifies how trauma can manifest as ultra-independence and perfectionism. When we first met via video call, she looked like she'd stepped out of a fashion magazine—not a hair out of place, designer outfit perfectly pressed, and flawless makeup. But this impeccable exterior was just the tip of the iceberg.

Alisha's childhood was chaotic. An alcoholic father with unpredictable outbursts and an emotionally distant mother taught her one clear lesson: the only person she could rely on was herself. Alisha concluded that if she could be perfect—if she could control every aspect of her life—maybe she could prevent the next crisis, the next disappointment, the next letdown.

This need for perfection followed Alisha into adulthood. Her home was always spotless, her work performance flawless. She'd wake up an hour early to ensure everything was in place before leaving for work. At the office, she was known as a high-achiever, but her colleagues found her difficult to work with.

"I once spent three hours reformatting a colleague's report," she told me, her voice a mix of pride and embarrassment. "I knew it wasn't my job, but I couldn't bear the thought of our team presenting something that wasn't absolutely perfect."

In her personal life, Alisha struggled to form close relationships. Her connections were superficial. Real, intimate friendships? Those were too risky. After all, getting close to someone meant they might see behind the perfect facade and discover she wasn't always strong, capable, and in control.

Breaking the Cycle: Alisha's Journey from Survival to Thriving

When Alisha first came to me, she was constantly on edge, her perfectionism and need for control exhausting her. It was clear she was stuck in survival mode. I remember telling her, "Alisha, you're not doomed to live like this forever. Our brains are incredibly adaptable, and with effort, we can rewire your nervous system to break free from trauma's grip."

I saw a glimmer of hope in her eyes, quickly followed by skepticism. "But how?" she asked.

We started by acknowledging the experiences from her past that had led to her ultra-independence. I helped her understand that while her childhood chaos had shaped her behaviors, our job now was to look forward and find new ways of being.

Our first session focused on diaphragmatic breathing. Before we began, I explained the role of the vagus nerve to Alisha. "The vagus nerve is like a communication highway between your brain and your body," I said. "It's a crucial part of your body's relaxation system. When we breathe deeply, we're essentially activating this nerve, telling our body to relax and that everything's okay."

Alisha looked intrigued. "So, breathing can actually change how my body responds to stress?" she asked.

"Exactly," I nodded. "When we activate the vagus nerve through deep breathing, it helps shift us from 'fight or flight' mode to 'rest and digest' mode."

With this understanding, I guided Alisha through the process of diaphragmatic breathing. At first, she struggled to slow her breathing, her chest barely moving as she took shallow breaths. But as she focused on activating her vagus nerve, she began to relax, her shoulders visibly dropping.

"I can actually feel the difference," she said after a few minutes, surprise evident in her voice.

In our next few sessions, we worked on progressive muscle relaxation. I watched as Alisha tensed and relaxed different muscle groups, her brow furrowed in concentration. "This is another way to send calming signals through your vagus nerve," I explained. "We're telling your body it's safe to relax."

Mindfulness meditation was challenging for Alisha at first. "I can't shut off my brain," she complained. So we started small, just five minutes a day. I taught her to focus on her breath, and when her mind wandered, to gently bring it back without judgment. Slowly but surely, Alisha began to find moments of peace in her meditation practice.

One particularly stressful day, Alisha called me in a panic. I talked her through a sensory grounding exercise over the phone, guiding her to identify things she could see, touch, hear, smell, and taste. By the end of the call, Alisha's voice had lost its frantic edge. "I feel...present," she said, sounding almost surprised. "And calmer. Is this the vagus nerve at work too?"

"Yes," I confirmed. "Grounding exercises help activate the vagus nerve by bringing you into the present moment and out of the stress response."

Perhaps the biggest challenge was getting Alisha to incorporate regular physical exercise into her routine. "I don't have time," was her constant refrain. So we brainstormed ways to make movement fun and accessible. Alisha discovered she loved dancing, and soon she was taking regular dance breaks throughout her day. "It's become my stress release," she told me, a genuine smile in her voice.

Over time, I watched as Alisha's nervous system began to regulate. The constant tension in her body eased, and she started to approach life with more flexibility and less fear. She was no longer living in constant survival mode but learning to thrive.

One day, Alisha came to our session looking relaxed - her hair in a messy bun, wearing jeans and a t-shirt. She smiled sheepishly and said, "I figured it was time to let you see the real me, messy parts and all." That's when I knew we'd turned a corner. Alisha was no longer hiding behind a facade of perfection but embracing her whole self - imperfections and all. Her vagus nerve - and her entire nervous system - had learned a new, more relaxed way of being.

Time for Some Reflection:

Before we wrap up, let's do a little self-reflection.

Exercise 1: Your Go-To Stress Response:

Take a minute to think about which of these responses (fight, flight, freeze, or fawn) you usually default to when stress hits. How might this tie into experiences from your past? Jot down your thoughts—no judgment, just curiosity.

Exercise 2: Your Ultra-Independence Inventory:

Take a look at your ultra-independent behaviors.

Here's a list to get you started—check off the ones that resonate with you, and feel free to add your own:

- Difficulty asking for help, even when overwhelmed.

- Overworking or being a "workaholic".

- Perfectionism in tasks or appearance.

- Trouble delegating tasks to others.

- Difficulty expressing emotions or being vulnerable.

- Always being the "problem solver" for friends and family.

- Reluctance to rely on partners or close friends.

- Avoiding commitments or long-term relationships.

- Insistence on financial independence, even in partnerships.

- Difficulty accepting compliments or praise.

- Tendency to isolate when stressed.

- Reluctance to share decision-making with others.

- Always having a "plan B" (or C, D, E...)

- Difficulty receiving care when sick or injured.

Now, pick 2-3 behaviors that stand out to you the most. For each one, reflect on these questions:

- When did this behavior first appear in your life? Can you remember a specific incident?

- What need was it trying to meet? (Safety? Control? Approval? Something else?)

- How does it serve you now? (Consider both positive and negative impacts)

- What might it feel like to loosen your grip on this behavior, just a little bit.

Exercise 3: Self-Compassion Letter:

Write a letter to yourself from the perspective of a loving, compassionate friend. What would they say about your struggles? How would they encourage you?

Remember, we're not here to judge these behaviors. They've helped you survive and thrive. But perhaps some of them have outlived their usefulness. It's all about finding that sweet spot between independence and connection.

Take your time with this. There's no right or wrong answer—it's all about understanding yourself better. And hey, give yourself a pat on the back for doing this work. Self-reflection isn't easy, but it's incredibly valuable.

Moving Forward with Your Insights

Now that you've reflected on your stress responses, ultra-independent behaviors, and shown yourself some compassion, it's time to think about how you can use these insights going forward. Here are a few suggestions:

- Notice your patterns: When you find yourself in stressful situations, try to observe which of the Four F responses you're defaulting to. Just noticing can be a powerful first step in changing patterns.

- Practice small acts of vulnerability: If you identified difficulty asking for help as one of your behaviors, challenge yourself to ask for assistance with something small. It could be as simple as asking a coworker for their opinion on a project.

- Experiment with letting go: Choose one of your ultra-independent behaviors and experiment with loosening your grip on it. For example, if you always need to be in control, try delegating a small task to someone else.

- Continue with relaxation practices: Whether it's deep breathing, meditation, or physical exercise, make time for activities that help regulate your nervous system.

Remember, change doesn't happen overnight. Be patient with yourself as you navigate this journey from survival to thriving. Every small step is progress.

In the next chapter, we're going to dig into the family photo album. It's like your great-grandma's china set, but instead of dishes, it's patterns of behavior being passed down. We'll explore how Uncle Joe's stiff upper lip and Grandma's "I can do it all myself" attitude might have trickled down to shape your own brand of independence.

Chapter Five

Breaking Generational Patterns

In breaking the chains of generational conditioning, we discover the true freedom of receiving and our own boundless potential.

Tamzin's Story: The Weight of Inheritance

Tamzin stands in front of her dressing table mirror, methodically applying concealer to the dark circles under her eyes. The clock reads 5:30 AM - another day, another early start. As she works, her eyes drift to the faded photograph tucked into the corner of the mirror frame.

Three generations of Novak women stare back at her: her grandmother Eliza, stern-faced in a nurse's uniform from the old country; her mother Irina, a teenager with wary eyes and a forced smile; and baby Tamzin, held stiffly in her grandmother's arms.

Tamzin's fingers brush the photo, tracing the line of women who came before her. She remembers her mother's voice, soft but firm: "We came to this country with nothing but the clothes on our backs, Tamzin. Trust no one but family. Work hard. Never show weakness."

The sound of her pager jolts her back to the present. A voicemail from the hospital - emergency surgery needed. Without hesitation, Tamzin grabs her keys and heads out, leaving behind a half-empty apartment and an unmade bed.

At the hospital, Tamzin moves with practiced efficiency, her face a mask of calm competence. A nurse approaches, clipboard in hand. "Dr. Novak, I have some concerns about-"

"I'll handle it," Tamzin cuts her off, not unkindly but firmly. She doesn't need help. Novak women always manage on their own.

Hours later, post-surgery, Tamzin sits alone in the doctors' lounge, a cold cup of coffee untouched before her. Her colleagues chat and laugh in the corner, but she remains apart, an invisible barrier separating her from their camaraderie.

Her phone buzzes - a text from her mother. "Working late again? Good girl. Dinner on Sunday, don't forget."

Tamzin's thumb hovers over the reply button. For a moment, she considers typing "I'm tired, Mom. Sometimes I wish..." But the words die unformed. Instead, she sends back a simple "OK."

As she leaves the hospital, the weight of expectations heavy on her shoulders, Tamzin passes the maternity ward. Through the window, she sees a new mother cradling her baby, tears of joy streaming down her face. The woman's own mother stands beside her, arms wrapped protectively around them both.

Something stirs in Tamzin's chest - a longing, a question. What would it be like to break the cycle? To trust, to lean on others, to show vulnerability?

But as quickly as the thought comes, she pushes it away. She is a Novak woman. Strong. Independent. Alone.

Tamzin straightens her back and walks on, the echoes of generations past guiding her steps. The pattern holds, unbroken. For now.

Rinse, lather, repeat

Imagine your great-grandma's emotional baggage morphing into your grandma's anxieties, which then become your mom's coping mechanisms. And now? Those same issues are popping up in your life as trust issues. Not exactly the inheritance we were hoping for, huh?

These inherited patterns can be stubborn as hell, like old family heirlooms we can't seem to get rid of. Maybe your dad struggled to show emotions because of his traumatic past, and now you find yourself doing the same dance. Or perhaps you keep attracting toxic partners, mirroring your mom's relationship history.

But recognizing these patterns gives us the power to change them. It's like realizing you've been wearing your grandma's outdated glasses and finally getting a new prescription. Clarity, at last!

The Science Behind the Inheritance: Epigenetics

Let's talk about a fascinating field of study called epigenetics. At its core, epigenetics reveals how our ancestors' emotions and experiences can be passed down to us through modifications to our DNA.

For example, imagine your great-grandparents lived through a war, experiencing intense fear and hardship. Epigenetics suggests that the trauma they endured didn't just affect them psychologically; it actually influenced how their genes were expressed. These altered genetic expressions were then passed down through generations, potentially manifesting as anxiety or heightened stress responses in you, even though you never experienced the original traumatic events.

It's not just negative experiences that can be inherited. If your ancestors lived through times of abundance and joy, you might have inherited a predisposition towards optimism or resilience.

The exciting part about epigenetics is that it's not set in stone. While we might inherit certain tendencies or predispositions, we have the power to influence how these genes express themselves. Through positive experiences, mindfulness practices, and self-care, we can actually reshape our genetic expression.

This means that while we may have inherited some challenging traits, we also have the ability to rewrite our genetic story. By understanding this science, we gain insight into why we might feel or behave in certain ways, and more importantly, we learn that we have the power to change these patterns.

Epigenetics gives us a transformative perspective: we are influenced by our ancestral past, but we are not bound by it. We can honor our ancestors' experiences while also creating new, healthier patterns for ourselves and future generations.

The Healing Power of Understanding and Empathy

Breaking free from generational cycles isn't about finding one magic solution. It's more like a blend of science, soul-searching, and connecting with something bigger than ourselves. We're all standing on the shoulders of giants - our ancestors. Those women who came before us? They were tough as nails, even when life was serving them lemons without the sugar.

Step one in this healing journey? Acknowledging that great-great-grandma's unresolved issues are living rent-free in your psyche. It's about saying, "I see you, ancestral trauma, and I'm ready to tackle you for myself and future generations."

Next up is compassion - for ourselves and our ancestors. Try shifting from blame to understanding. Our ancestors faced some tough stuff and did their best with the tools they had. This perspective shift opens the door to empathy, bridging past and present while stretching into the future.

Understanding their struggles is like finding the key to understanding ourselves. We can take their strengths - their resilience, their wisdom, their ability to make something out of nothing - and use these as building blocks for a better future.

Emotional Alchemy: Turning Lead into Gold

As we work on this generational healing, we're breaking patterns that have held us back for way too long. With newfound self-awareness, we start rewriting the narrative we've been telling ourselves forever. It's like editing our own life script, and let me tell you, it feels so good.

But the healing doesn't stop with us. We're throwing a pebble into a pond, and those ripples? They're spreading out to our families and communities. When we break free from generational trauma, we're basically shouting from the rooftops, "Hey, healing is possible!"

We're often lugging around the weight of family histories, cultural expectations, and societal conditioning like overpacked suitcases. These generational patterns? They're puppet masters, pulling the strings of our beliefs and behaviors around receiving help, trust, and emotional intelligence. And if you're part of a marginalized group? That's a whole extra layer of complexity.

An Ancestral Discovery Session

During an ancestral discovery session with one of my clients, we uncovered some fascinating family history. My client was having a tough time letting romance into her life.

As we delved into her past, we discovered some remarkable stories. Her great-grandmother became a widow way too young and then decided to pack up and move to the USA. Now, we're not talking about hopping on a quick flight. This was a boat journey that took months, and she did it alone with her baby daughter. Can you imagine? Arriving in a foreign country, probably not speaking the language, with a baby on your hip and no husband in sight. Talk about brave!

This great-grandma never remarried. Her daughter - our client's grandmother - became a successful legal secretary but also raised her children on her own after her marriage ended. And then there's the client's mother, who has been through multiple unsuccessful relationships and now refuses to date at all.

So here is my client, never married and struggling to form relationships. She has an "I can do it all myself" attitude that may have intimidated previous partners. But during our session, we saw how her family history molded her into an incredibly strong and self-sufficient person. However, it also made it difficult for her to let others in and accept help or vulnerability.

But she had no idea about her great-grandmother's incredible journey. In a time where women traveling alone was rare, imagine the rarity of a woman traveling with a baby. It was like being a real-life superhero.

In our session, we looked at how this family history shaped her into an incredibly strong and self-sufficient woman. We're talking about resilience that can weather any storm, courage that could put a lion to shame, and inner strength that could move mountains. We also explored the downside - how it may have made it difficult for her to let others in, ask for help, or believe that anyone could keep up with her.

It was like witnessing a lightbulb flicker on over her head. She began to see how these impressive women had unknowingly passed down both their strengths and struggles to her.

This session wasn't about erasing all of that independence; rather, it was about finding harmony - honoring the power of her ancestors while learning to accept help, be vulnerable, and allow others in when needed.

Honoring Our Ancestral Strengths

Let's pause and recognize something amazing: our ancestors have gifted us with some incredible strengths, resilience, and positive traits. Some of these might be flying under your radar.

Consider this: the mere fact that you are here, reading this book, is a testament to the survival skills, adaptability, and fortitude inherited from those who came before you.

Maybe your grandma's tenacity in the face of adversity shows up in your own determination to crush your goals. Perhaps your great-grandpa's curiosity about the world has morphed into your love for binge-watching documentaries. Or it could be that your aunt's infectious laughter has shaped your ability to find joy in the small stuff.

I used to get super irritated with my mom. She would tell a story but exaggerate it, not lie, just fluff it up with extra bells and whistles. All my life this drove me crazy until I realized that this was her knack for storytelling, and she would have done well to write a book. And actually, I inherited that fluffy storytelling gift, and now I can use it to write stories with all the fluff and bells and whistles.

Walking in the Footsteps of Those Before Me

Growing up, I had little knowledge of my paternal family's history. All I knew was that my grandparents fled their homeland in Eastern Europe for South Africa during the 1930s to escape the looming threat of war. In 2019, I embarked on a journey to Lithuania to uncover my roots.

Knowing very little about the location, I took a leap and booked a hotel online. As fate would have it, I found myself at the entrance of an old village that held significance for my ancestors. For two weeks, I explored the streets and sat on benches that were older than my own relatives, trying to decipher foreign signs and symbols.

I also visited Paneriai Forest, a site where thousands of innocent people were tragically killed during the early 1940s. The weight of this dark history hung heavy on my heart. At first, it all felt distant—like something I was not part of. But as my trip progressed, I started to feel a deep connection growing within me to the land and its people.

It was as if I could feel my ancestors' energy coursing through me as I walked down the same streets they once called home, sensing their love for this country and their grief at having to leave it behind. When it was time for me to return home, I felt both exhausted and renewed—like I had just undergone an intense therapy session with my ancestors.

This experience was profound beyond words, allowing me to connect with my family's past in ways I never thought possible. If you ever have the chance to visit your ancestral homelands, seize it without hesitation. You may be surprised by what you discover.

It's not just about tracing your lineage; it's about feeling the roots that anchor you to your past and finding resilience in the legacy they have left behind. My journey taught me that our family stories are more than just mere tales from the past—they are alive and intertwined with our own identities. By following in their footsteps, we can begin to unravel the intricate tapestry of our heritage and find strength in the enduring legacy they have left behind.

Exploring Your Roots: Practical Exercises:

1. Make a family tree and note dominant emotions or patterns for each family member.

2. Chat with your older relatives. They've got stories, and probably some juicy gossip too.

3. Look through old family photos. You might discover your grandma was a total fashion icon.

4. Visit places your ancestors lived. It's like time travel, but without the DeLorean.

5. Try out some family recipes. Warning: may result in unexpected emotions and/or indigestion.

6. Read old letters or journals. It's like Facebook stalking, but vintage.

7. Check yourself out in the mirror and spot those inherited traits.

Diving Deeper: Reflection Exercises:

Exercise 1: Family Message Deep Dive:

What messages did you get growing up about being strong, capable, or successful? How have these shaped your beliefs about receiving help and being independent?

Exercise 2: Community Love Reflection:

Think about a time when you felt truly seen and accepted by a community. What made that experience so nourishing?

Exercise 3: Emotional Intelligence Check-In:

How comfortable are you with identifying and expressing your own emotions and needs? How about tuning into others' emotions?

Exercise 4: Marginalization Impact:

Reflect on your experiences of marginalization or oppression. How have these shaped your sense of trust and safety in the world?

Exercise 5: Ancestral Pattern Shift:

Identify one family pattern or belief around receiving help that you'd like to change. What new story could you tell yourself about your worthiness to receive?

Exercise 6: Discovering Your Ancestral Strengths:

Make a list of at least 10 family members and identify one unique strength or positive trait for each person. Reflect on how you might have inherited or learned from each of these strengths.

Embracing Your Ancestral Strength and Forging Your Path

Remember, you come from a long line of survivors, healers, and total badasses. Your own journey towards growth and transformation is an important part of that legacy. Trust in your own inner wisdom and let it guide you on this path of receiving, faith, and emotional intelligence.

Healing is a continuous journey, not a final destination. It's okay to take small steps forward, make mistakes, and get back up again. Embrace the messiness, imperfections, and occasional tears. And don't forget to laugh at yourself and the absurdity of it all.

As you continue exploring your family patterns and ancestral strengths, you may find yourself at a crossroads. On one hand, you want to honor your roots and the resilience of those who came before you. On the other hand, you need to create your own path and break free from limiting beliefs and behaviors.

This is where setting boundaries becomes crucial. Boundaries are not walls that shut others out; they are clear lines that define where you end and others begin. They are essential tools for maintaining your identity while still engaging in meaningful relationships.

In the next chapter, we'll delve into the courage it takes to establish healthy boundaries - both with our families and ourselves.

So, my strong friend, as you finish this chapter, take a moment to acknowledge how far you've come. You are doing the work of generations - not just healing yourself but creating ripples of change that will impact your family for years to come. Inhale the strength of your ancestors, exhale the patterns that no longer serve you, and prepare to discover the power of your own voice and boundaries.

The journey continues, and the best is yet to come.

You've got this!

Chapter Six

Setting Boundaries

Boundaries are not walls to keep others out, but paths that guide us to healthier, more authentic connections.

Mia's Story: The Ultra-Independent Struggle with Boundaries

Mia pastes on a polite smile as her high-maintenance client, Frankie, drones on about needing more website revisions by tomorrow's meeting. She can feel her jaw clenching at the totally unreasonable demand.

Does he not get that she's already working around the clock to keep up with his constantly changing design feedback? And that's on top of juggling three other client projects and managing her own small agency.

Mia's struggle with boundaries is a classic example of the challenges faced by ultra-independent women. Her ability to handle multiple clients, manage her own agency, and work around the clock is a testament to her self-reliance. Yet, this same ultra-independence makes it difficult for her to set and maintain healthy boundaries. She's so accustomed to doing it all that the idea of limiting what she takes on feels almost like a personal failure.

A part of Mia wants to cut Frankie off and lay down some firm boundaries. She's bent over backward trying to make this partnership work, but he keeps taking her flexibility for granted, chipping away at her time and sanity with his relentless demands.

But an even bigger part of Mia cringes at the thought of potentially disappointing Frankie or losing his business altogether. She has vivid memories of how her single mom's inability to hold firm boundaries with sketchy tenants and abusive partners had kept them stuck in a cycle of instability and struggle during her childhood.

"We have to take whatever we can get from people," her mother would say whenever Mia complained about the latest violation of their well-being. "Beggars can't be choosers in this world."

So at a bone-deep level, Mia absorbed the belief that standing up for her reasonable limits or self-worth meant risking the little security they had. Better to just go along with things, to mold herself into an endlessly accommodating shape to avoid conflict or scarcity.

"Sure, Frankie, I can have those tweaks ready for you," she hears herself say in an artificially upbeat tone. "Just let me know if there's anything else you need."

As soon as the words leave her mouth, Mia feels her throat tighten with self-betrayal. There it is again—her fear of saying "no" paving the way for others to steamroll her boundaries and autonomy. She's already dreading the inevitably late night ahead, feeling the familiar pangs of resentment toward Frankie even before he's hung up the call.

The Ultra-Independent Paradox: Boundaryless and Overburdened

Mia's story probably sounds familiar to many ultra-independent women. We've spent our lives learning to go it alone, handling whatever comes our way through sheer force of self-reliance. The idea of drawing lines around our time, energy, or values and communicating them clearly to others? That feels perilously close to admitting we can't do it all, that we have limits and needs of our own.

But here's the paradox: our ultra-independence, while a source of strength, can also leave us vulnerable to overextension and burnout if we don't learn to set boundaries. Boundaries aren't just important—they're essential for our well-being and success, especially for those of us who pride ourselves on our self-sufficiency. Let's explore why, and how we can start setting them, even when it feels terrifying.

The Power of Personal Boundaries

So, what exactly are these boundaries, and why are they so powerful? Think of boundaries as invisible lines that protect our emotional, physical, intellectual, and spiritual selves. They help us communicate our core values, how we want to be treated, and what we absolutely need to feel safe and respected.

At their core, boundaries protect who we are—our integrity, sovereignty, and inherent worthiness. They create the space to fully be ourselves, without twisting ourselves into knots to gain approval or avoid guilt and shame. Essentially, boundaries allow us to bring our whole, authentic selves to every aspect of our lives.

For Mia, setting boundaries might look like:

- Clearly communicating her working hours to clients and sticking to them.

- Establishing a project change policy that respects her time and expertise.

- Learning to say no to clients or projects that don't align with her values or available bandwidth.

These aren't arbitrary rules—they're guideposts that allow Mia to show up as her best self, both for her clients and for herself. For ultra-independent women like Mia, these boundaries can feel like a challenge to their capability, but they're actually a tool to enhance and sustain that capability.

The Hidden Cost of Boundarylessness for the Ultra-Independent

Living without boundaries comes at a high price, especially for ultra-independent women. We become drained by the unrealistic demands of others and, worse, by the unrealistic demands we place on ourselves. We allow our core values to be compromised. We lose touch with our deepest needs and priorities in the endless quest to prove our sufficiency to the world.

Our ability to handle multiple responsibilities and challenges can lead others to place unrealistic demands on us, and worse, can lead us to place unrealistic demands on ourselves. We allow our core values to be compromised in the name of proving we can do it all.

I see this pattern play out with clients all the time. Take Jackie, a brilliant marketing executive. Jackie came to me burned out and on the verge of quitting her dream job. "I was told that I was selfish when I tried to tell my mother what I wanted," she shared, "so I never say anything because I don't want to be viewed as selfish."

This early message made it challenging for Jackie to express her needs or desires, both personally and professionally. She'd take on every project, work late into the night, and never ask for help—all while slowly drowning in overwhelm and resentment. Her ultra-independence, once a source of pride, had become a trap.

The Boundary-Self-Esteem Connection: A Challenge for the Ultra-Independent

Here's something interesting: the relationship between boundaries and self-esteem is profound and reciprocal. By establishing and upholding healthy boundaries, we're not only communicating our self-respect to others but also to ourselves. On the flip side, having a strong sense of self-worth allows us to effectively set and maintain boundaries with others.

For ultra-independent women, this connection can be complex. Our self-worth is often tied to our ability to handle everything on our own. Setting boundaries might initially feel like admitting weakness or failure. However, it's crucial to understand that boundaries are not a sign of weakness, but a tool for maintaining our strength and independence in a healthy way.

Think about it: every time Mia says yes to Frankie's unreasonable demands, she's inadvertently sending herself the message that her time, expertise, and well-being are less important than keeping a difficult client happy. Over time, this erodes her self-esteem and leads to deepening resentment.

By contrast, when we honor our boundaries, we validate our own experiences and needs, boosting our sense of self-worth. It's a self-reinforcing cycle that can actually enhance our independence by making it more sustainable.

Breaking the People-Pleasing Pattern

One of the biggest hurdles ultra-independent women face in setting boundaries is the deeply ingrained habit of people-pleasing. We develop intense fears that saying "no" to any request will lead to rejection, abandonment, or being ostracized from the "inner circle." Our worthiness gets tangled up in relentless people-pleasing patterns.

I used to be the queen of people-pleasing. I always thought I had boundaries, but I didn't at all. My incessant need to keep the peace and make everyone happy meant I was always saying yes. This applied to friends, relationships, family, and work.

It took me a long time to understand that boundaries work both ways. Take, for example, my lack of financial boundaries. I spent decades paying for other people. We'd go out for dinner, and I'd pick up the tab. Why did I do this? Because I didn't want things to be awkward, and I saw myself as the independent superhero who could handle the expenses more easily than everyone else.

This led to many people taking advantage of me. On my side, I lacked boundaries in being able to say no when someone wanted me to pay or asked for money. On their side, they lacked boundaries in understanding that they couldn't just take from others.

It's a common pattern among ultra-independent women. We spend so many years in a fawn response, people-pleasing to fit in, feel included, and avoid upsetting the apple cart. While this may temporarily preserve a sense of likability and external validation, it comes at a profound cost.

The Journey to Healthy Boundaries

So how do we break free from these deeply ingrained patterns? How do we start setting and maintaining healthy boundaries? It's a journey, and like any journey, it starts with a single step.

For Mia, that first step came the day after her late-night work session for Frankie. Exhausted and resentful, she realized something had to change. She couldn't keep operating this way and expect different results.

She drafted an email to Frankie, outlining her new project change policy and working hours. She explained that while she valued their working relationship, the current arrangement wasn't sustainable. She offered clear alternatives that respected both his needs as a client and her needs as a business owner.

As her finger hovered over the send button, all her old fears surfaced. What if he got angry? What if he fired her? What if this ruined everything she'd worked so hard to build?

But then she remembered something we'd discussed in our coaching sessions: "Your 'no' is a sacred 'yes' to something else." By saying no to Frankie's unreasonable demands, she was saying yes to her own well-being, to sustainable success, to showing up as her best self for all her clients.

She took a deep breath and hit send.

Practical Steps for Setting Boundaries

Mia's journey to setting boundaries is just beginning, and so is yours. Here are some practical steps you can take to start setting and maintaining healthy boundaries:

- **Identify Your Limits:** Take some time to reflect on what you can and cannot tolerate in your relationships, work, and daily life. What makes you feel uncomfortable or resentful?

- **Be Clear and Direct:** When communicating your boundaries, be specific and straightforward. Instead of "I don't know if I can make it to your party," try "Thank you for the invitation, but I won't be able to attend."

- **Use "I" Statements:** Express your boundaries in terms of your own feelings and needs, rather than accusing or blaming others. For example, "I feel overwhelmed when I receive last-minute requests. I need more notice to manage my workload effectively."

- **Start Small:** If setting boundaries feels overwhelming, start with something small in a low-stakes situation. As you build confidence, you can tackle bigger issues.

- **Expect Pushback:** Some people may not respond well to your new boundaries at first. That's okay. Stay firm and remember that you're doing this for your well-being.

Remember, setting boundaries is a skill, and like any skill, it takes practice. Be patient with yourself as you learn and grow.

The Digital Frontier: Setting Boundaries in a Connected World

In our hyper-connected age, it's more important than ever to set clear boundaries around our online presence and communications.

Here are some strategies Mia implemented, which you might find helpful too:

- **Defined Work Hours:** Mia set up an auto-responder for her work email, clearly stating her working hours and when clients could expect a response.

- **Social Media Limits:** She decided to limit her social media use to certain hours of the day, helping her stay focused and reducing digital overwhelm.

- **Notification Management:** Mia turned off non-essential notifications on her phone, allowing her to be more present in her daily life.

- **Digital Detox:** She implemented a weekly "digital detox" day, where she disconnected from all devices and focused on in-person interactions and personal activities.

Remember, these digital boundaries are just as important as your real-world ones. They protect your time, your energy, and your peace of mind.

The Ripple Effect of Healthy Boundaries

As Mia continued to work on setting and maintaining boundaries, she noticed something remarkable happening. Yes, there was initial pushback from some clients, and yes, it felt uncomfortable at times. But overall, her relationships—both professional and personal—began to improve.

Clients who truly valued her work respected her new policies. She found herself doing better work in less time because she was no longer constantly interrupted or overextended. Her resentment faded, replaced by a renewed passion for her work.

Even more surprisingly, Mia found that setting boundaries in her professional life gave her the courage to do the same in her personal life. She started saying no to social obligations that drained her, making more time for the relationships and activities that truly nourished her.

This is the ripple effect of setting healthy boundaries. When we honor our own needs and limits, we show up more fully and authentically in all areas of our lives. We model healthy behavior for others. We create space for genuine connection and mutual respect.

Your Ultra-Independent Boundary-Setting Journey

As we wrap up this chapter, I want you to remember something important: for ultra-independent women, setting boundaries is not about diminishing your strength or self-reliance. It's about channeling that independence in a way that sustains you, rather than depletes you. It's about creating the conditions that allow you to show up as your best self, to do your best work, and to foster genuine, respectful relationships - all while maintaining the independence that is core to who you are.

Your journey to setting healthy boundaries, like Mia's, is just beginning. There will be challenges along the way. You might be shocked by people's reactions to the new, boundary-setting version of you. Some friendships might diminish, people might get angry at first, and they might say things like, "Why have you changed? You used to do this for me."

It's important to understand that these reactions are normal. People have grown accustomed to your boundaryless behavior, and change can be uncomfortable for them. They will either get used to your new boundaries or they will drift away. Frankly, if they only liked you when you did everything they wanted, those weren't healthy relationships to begin with. It's okay to let go of those friendships.

You might slip back into old patterns sometimes, and that's okay. Remember, progress, not perfection, is the goal. Each time you maintain a boundary, you're strengthening your self-respect and teaching others how to treat you.

As you move forward, keep these final thoughts in mind:

- Your needs matter: You are not selfish for having needs and limits. You deserve respect and consideration.

- Boundaries are an act of self-love: By setting boundaries, you're taking care of yourself and showing others how to treat you.

- It gets easier with practice: Like any skill, setting and maintaining boundaries becomes more natural with time.

- You're not alone: Remember, countless other women are on this journey with you. Seek support when you need it.

- Your 'no' is a 'yes' to something else: Every time you set a boundary, you're creating space for something that truly matters to you.

- Expect and accept changes in relationships: As you set boundaries, some relationships may change or end. This is a natural part of the process and makes room for healthier connections.

Identifying Personal Values and Informing Boundary-Setting

This exercise will help you identify your values and consider how they inform your boundaries:

Value Exploration:

From this list of values, choose 5 which truly resonate with you.

Honesty

Kindness

Growth

Freedom

Creativity

Family

Achievement

Health

Adventure

Integrity

Respect

Harmony

Justice

Wisdom

Compassion

Security

Love

Courage

Independence

Teamwork

The most important thing is that the values you choose truly reflect what's important to you.

Value Definition:

For each of your top 5 values, write a brief description of what it means to you personally.

Value in Action:

- For each value, list 2-3 ways you currently express this value in your life.

- Now, identify 2-3 ways you could express this value more fully.

Boundary Alignment:

For each value, consider:

- What boundaries might support living this value more fully?

- Are there any current situations where this value is being compromised?

- What new boundary could you set to honor this value?

Practical Application:

- Choose one value-aligned boundary to focus on implementing this week.

- Write specific actions you'll take to establish and maintain this boundary.

Reflection:

At the end of the week, reflect on your experience:

- How did it feel to set this boundary?

- What challenges did you face?

- How did honoring this boundary align with your values?

Boundary Reflection Exercises:

Exercise 1: Boundary Struggles:

What type of boundary gives you the most grief? Is it saying no to extra work, or maybe setting limits with family? What's the little voice in your head saying that makes it so hard?

Exercise 2: Boundary Wishlist:

If you could wave a magic wand, where would you love to have stronger boundaries? Maybe it's not checking work emails on weekends, or not letting your mom guilt-trip you. Jot down 5-10 ideas.

Exercise 3: Rewrite the Script:

Take a couple of those boundary wishes and rephrase them in a way that makes you feel empowered. Instead of "I can't help my friend move every single weekend," try "I value my free time, so I'm only available to help once a month." See how much better that feels?

Exercise 4: Learn from the Oops:

Think about a time you let your boundaries slide and regretted it. How did it make you feel? What did it teach you about sticking to your guns in the future?

Exercise 5: Your Boundary Squad:

Who are the people in your life who've got your back when it comes to boundaries? List 5 friends, family members, or mentors you could turn to for support or advice. Bonus points if you can think of someone who's really good at boundaries - what could you learn from them?

Now that we've laid the groundwork for setting healthy boundaries, let's zoom in on one of the trickiest areas to apply them - family. In the next chapter, we'll explore how to navigate the complex web of family dynamics while maintaining our newfound boundary-setting skills.

Chapter Seven

Family Dynamics

Family can be both our deepest wound and our greatest challenge to heal. It's where we learned our strength, and where we must learn to be vulnerable again.

Linda's Story: Stuck in the Middle

It's 2 AM, and Linda's phone is buzzing like an angry hornet. She knows it's her mom before she even looks. With a groan, she picks up, bracing herself for the inevitable drama tsunami.

"Linda, darling, I need you here now," her mom's voice slices through the night. "Can't find my pills, and my back's killing me. You know I'm helpless without you."

Linda's exhausted to her bones, but she's already throwing on clothes. This is the second midnight emergency this week alone. It's a dance she knows all too well - her mom relying on her for every little thing while simultaneously tearing her to shreds with criticism sharper than a surgeon's scalpel.

Growing up, Linda's mom was a real piece of work. Nothing Linda did was ever good enough. Try to set a boundary? Cue the guilt trips thick enough to choke on. "After all I've done for you, this is the thanks I get?" her mom would wail, voice dripping with contempt.

So Linda became the ultimate people-pleaser, a human sponge soaking up all of mom's toxic energy. Now, as an adult with her own family, she's still trapped in this messed-up cycle. Her mom's grip is titanium-strong, and Linda's suffocating under the weight of it all.

As she drives to her mom's house, resentment bubbles up like lava. She loves her mom fiercely, but this relationship is eating her alive. She's neglecting her own family, her job, her sanity - all in the name of being a "good daughter."

But what does that even mean when your mom's constantly tearing you down? How do you set boundaries with someone who's trampled them all your life? Linda's drowning in an ocean of obligation and guilt.

She knows something's got to give, but the thought of standing up to her mom fills her with terror. What if mom cuts her off completely? What if she's not strong enough to weather the storm?

Pulling into the driveway, Linda takes a deep breath, armoring up for the inevitable barrage. She knows this can't go on forever, but she's not sure how to take that first step towards healing.

For now, she'll do what she's always done - slap on a brave face, handle mom's drama, and try to silence that little voice screaming for something more. But deep down, Linda knows that someday, something's got to change. She just hopes she's got the guts to face it when it does.

Linda's story is a prime example of how our childhood experiences shape who we become. Our views about ourselves are heavily influenced by the family dynamics we were exposed to as children. Our brain forms a filter based on those early experiences, shaping our perception of ourselves and the world around us. Even when we realize that these patterns do not serve us well, they can be difficult to break free from. To understand why this is, we must explore the fascinating realm of our brain's belief system filter.

What We Are Programmed to Believe: Understanding our Reticular Activating System (RAS)

Our brains are incredible organs, the most complex and advanced operating system out there, constantly processing an overwhelming amount of information from our environment. But how does our brain decide what information is important enough to bring to our conscious attention? This is where the Reticular Activating System (RAS) comes into play.

Think of your RAS as your brain's personal assistant, tirelessly working behind the scenes to filter the constant stream of information you encounter. It decides what gets VIP access to your conscious mind based on what it believes is important to you. And those beliefs are largely shaped by your experiences, especially those early family interactions we all go through.

Once programmed, your belief system (which we'll use interchangeably with RAS throughout this chapter) acts like a pair of tinted glasses, coloring your perception of the world to confirm your existing beliefs - whether they serve you or not. In Linda's case, her RAS has been programmed to constantly look for ways to please her mother and avoid criticism, even at the cost of her own well-being. This programming runs so deep that even the thought of change terrifies her.

Luckily, we can reprogram our RAS. Understanding how our belief system works is the first step towards reshaping it to support healthier patterns and relationships.

Before we move deeper into family dynamics, let's address something crucial: it's absolutely okay to acknowledge the damage caused by your family while still loving them. This isn't about villainizing our parents or siblings, but about understanding how our experiences have shaped us - and our RAS.

Many of us struggle with feelings of guilt when we begin to examine the impact our families have had on us. We may think, "But they did their best," or "It wasn't all bad." And that may be true - it's rare for it to be all bad. But acknowledging the difficult parts does not diminish the good, and it certainly doesn't mean we love our families any less. It simply means we are courageous enough to see the full picture, to honor our experiences, and to start the healing process by rewiring our belief systems.

Love and pain can coexist, and recognizing this is a significant step towards healing. Remember, this journey isn't about blame; it's about understanding and growth. Your RAS has been working overtime to protect you based on these early experiences - now it's time to teach it some new tricks.

The Mother of All Wounds: Mommy Issues 101

Now that we understand how our RAS shapes our perceptions, let's explore our first and most important connection - the one with our moms. This relationship plays a crucial role in programming our belief system, shaping how we see ourselves and interact with the world. For some, it's a source of strength. For others, it's the root of their ultra-independence.

Enter the "mother wound" - the emotional fallout from a difficult relationship with mom. Maybe she was physically absent, emotionally unavailable, or unpredictable. Whatever the case, it often leads to extreme self-reliance and programs our RAS to expect certain patterns in relationships.

Let's look at some real-life examples from my clients, and see how their experiences have shaped their belief systems:

The Distant Mom: Ava's Story

Ava's mom was physically there but emotionally absent. Always busy with work, she rarely engaged with Ava.

"I remember trying to show mom a drawing I made," Ava told me. "She barely looked up from her computer, just mumbled 'That's nice, honey' and kept typing. I felt invisible."

This emotional neglect taught Ava that she couldn't rely on others for support or validation. As an adult, she's become fiercely self-sufficient. "I never ask for help," she admits. "I've learned to do everything on my own because I don't trust anyone else to be there for me."

Ava's belief system was programmed to expect emotional unavailability from others. Her RAS constantly scans her environment for signs of rejection or disinterest, reinforcing her belief that she can only rely on herself.

The Helicopter Mom: Emma's Tale

Emma's mom was overly involved in every aspect of her life. Every decision needed mom's approval.

"I wanted to try out for the school play," Emma shares. "But mom insisted I focus on math club instead because it would 'look better on college applications.' I never got to explore my own interests."

This constant control paradoxically pushed Emma towards extreme independence in adulthood. "I make all my decisions alone now," she says. "I don't consult anyone because I'm terrified of losing my autonomy again. It's exhausting, but it feels safer than relying on others."

Emma's RAS was programmed to be hypervigilant about threats to her autonomy. Her belief system now constantly looks for situations where her independence might be compromised, even when collaboration could be beneficial.

The Drama Mama: Zoe's Experience

Zoe's childhood was unpredictable due to her mom's mood swings.

"One minute, Mom would be laughing with us, and the next, she'd be screaming over something tiny," Zoe remembers. "I became an expert at managing her emotions, always trying to keep the peace."

This led Zoe to become hyper-independent, believing she had to handle everything alone. "I don't share my problems with anyone," she explains. "I'm so used to being the fixer that I can't imagine leaning on others for support. It's lonely, but it feels safer than risking unpredictable reactions."

Zoe's belief system was programmed to constantly scan for potential emotional threats. Her RAS is always on high alert, looking for signs of mood changes in others and prompting Zoe to preemptively manage situations to avoid conflict.

These stories illustrate how our early experiences with our mothers can profoundly shape our belief systems and patterns of behavior. But mothers aren't the only influential figures in our family dynamics. Let's turn our attention to the impact of fathers on our RAS programming.

Who's Your Daddy? (Issues, That Is)

Just as our relationships with our mothers shape our RAS, growing up with a difficult father can also drive us towards ultra-independence and program our belief system in specific ways. Let's explore some examples from my clients:

The Absent Father: Debra's Journey

Debra's dad left when she was just three. This early abandonment shaped her approach to relationships and self-reliance.

"I always felt like I wasn't enough," Debra shares. "If I had been a better daughter, maybe he would have stayed. It's not logical, but that's how it felt."

This led Debra to become fiercely independent. "I never let anyone get close enough to leave me again," she admits. "I handle everything myself - my career, my home, my problems. It's exhausting, but it feels safer than depending on someone who might disappear."

Debra's belief system was programmed to expect abandonment. Her RAS constantly scans for signs that people might leave her, prompting her to maintain emotional distance as a form of self-protection.

The Critical Father: Jenna's Story

Jenna's dad was physically present but emotionally devastating. His constant criticism drove her towards perfectionism and self-reliance.

"I remember bringing home a report card full of A's and one B+," Jenna recalls. "All he said was, 'What happened in that class?' No praise for the A's, just focus on the one grade that wasn't perfect."

This led Jenna to become ultra-independent, always striving to prove her worth. "I never ask for help or admit weakness," she says. "I'm terrified that if I'm not perfect and completely self-sufficient, I'll be judged and found wanting. It's isolating, but it feels safer than risking criticism."

Jenna's RAS was programmed to constantly look for potential criticism or judgment. Her belief system filters her experiences to focus on any perceived failures or imperfections, reinforcing her belief that she must be perfect to be worthy.

The Volatile Father: Tasha's Tale

Tasha's dad had unpredictable mood swings that kept the family on edge. This volatility pushed Tasha towards extreme self-reliance.

"One minute, Dad would be joking around with us, and the next, he'd be yelling over something tiny," Tasha remembers. "We never knew what would set him off."

As a result, Tasha became hyper-independent. "I learned to anticipate and meet my own needs because relying on others felt dangerous," she explains. "I handle everything myself now - emotions, problems, decisions."

Tasha's belief system was programmed to be constantly on guard for potential emotional outbursts. Her RAS scans her environment for any signs of volatility, keeping her in a state of hyper-vigilance and self-reliance. This also influenced her choice in partners; Tasha subconsciously sought out men with volatile personalities like her father because her RAS led her to believe that love and volatility were inseparable.

These stories demonstrate how our relationships with our fathers can significantly influence our belief systems and behaviors. But our family dynamics aren't limited to our parents. Siblings also play a crucial role in shaping our RAS and patterns of independence.

The Relationship with Our Brothers and Sisters

Siblings play a crucial role in shaping our RAS and how we approach life as adults. They can influence us towards extreme self-reliance and program our RAS in distinct ways, making it essential to understand these dynamics in our families.

The Golden Child and Invisible Sibling: Alex's Story

Alex grew up feeling overshadowed by her sister Emma. Emma was the family star - straight A's, perfect hair, the whole package. Meanwhile, Alex felt overlooked.

"My parents weren't trying to be unfair," Alex told me. "They just had this endless enthusiasm for Emma's achievements. I felt like my accomplishments barely registered."

Living in Emma's shadow, Alex developed an intense drive to prove herself. She threw herself into her studies and career with fierce determination.

"I thought if I could just be successful enough, my parents would finally notice me," she admitted. "But no matter what I achieved, it never seemed to measure up."

This childhood dynamic led Alex to become ultra-independent. "I learned at a young age that I couldn't count on anyone else for validation or assistance," she shared. "This led me to become a people pleaser, constantly seeking approval and attention from others in order to make them happy."

Alex's belief system was programmed to constantly seek validation and recognition. Her RAS filters her experiences to focus on achievements and accomplishments, always looking for the next opportunity to prove her worth.

As we've seen through these various stories, our family dynamics play a crucial role in shaping our belief systems and patterns of independence. But understanding these patterns is just the first step. Now, let's explore how we can navigate these complex family relationships and start reprogramming our RAS for healthier interactions.

Navigating Family Dynamics: Finding Your Balance

Now that we've explored how our family experiences have shaped our belief systems, let's chat about how to handle these tricky family relationships when you're an ultra-independent woman. We're not aiming to completely heal generations of family drama (that's a whole other can of worms), but rather to understand our patterns, set some healthy boundaries, and start reprogramming our RAS.

First things first, let's talk about recognizing how your family has shaped you and your belief system.

Ask yourself:

- Do I sometimes catch myself acting just like my mom or dad?

- Do I become a different person around my family?

- Am I always the peacemaker, the rebel, or the invisible child in family gatherings?

- What patterns does my RAS seem to be focusing on in my family interactions?

Understanding these patterns is key because, let's face it, they have a sneaky way of showing up in other parts of our lives. You might find yourself playing the peacemaker at work or being the rebel in your romantic relationships without even realizing it. This is your RAS at work, applying the patterns it learned in your family to other areas of your life.

Now, let's talk boundaries. You've read the chapter on boundaries, so now it's time to put that knowledge into action with your family members.

Start small. Maybe it's deciding to limit calls with your overly demanding mom to once a week. Be clear and firm. And remember, "No" is a complete sentence. You don't owe anyone a lengthy explanation for your boundaries. As you set these boundaries, pay attention to how your belief system reacts. It might initially flag these changes as threats, based on old programming.

Self-care is non-negotiable, especially when dealing with family stuff. Schedule some alone time after family events to recharge. Have a go-to stress relief activity, whether it's meditation, a long run, or getting lost in a good book. And give yourself permission to leave situations that become too overwhelming. You're not being rude; you're taking care of yourself. This is also a great way to start reprogramming your RAS to prioritize your well-being.

Learning to communicate assertively is a game-changer. Express your needs and feelings without aggression or passivity. Try using "I" statements. Instead of "You always criticize me," try "I feel hurt when my achievements aren't recognized." This new way of communicating can help reprogram your belief system to expect more positive interactions.

If you've always been the family fixer or peacemaker, it's okay to step back. You're not responsible for managing everyone's emotions or solving every crisis. It's time to redefine your role in the family drama. This shift can help reprogram your RAS to stop constantly scanning for problems to solve.

And here's a radical thought: create your chosen family. Surround yourself with friends who support and understand you. It's perfectly okay if your biological family isn't your primary support system. This can help reprogram your belief system to expect positive, supportive relationships.

Remember, changing family dynamics and reprogramming your RAS is a process, not an overnight transformation. Be patient with yourself as you try out these strategies. It's okay to take two steps forward and one step back - what matters is that you're moving in the direction of healthier relationships and a more balanced independence.

Reprogramming Your Beliefs: The RAS Method

Now that we've explored various aspects of family dynamics and their impact on our belief systems, let's dive deeper into a powerful tool for change: the Reticular Activating System (RAS) reprogramming technique. This method is crucial for rewriting those deeply-rooted beliefs that were formed during childhood. These beliefs, which may have been influenced by our family and upbringing, can hinder our personal growth and ability to form healthy relationships.

Remember, the RAS is like your brain's personal assistant. It filters the massive amount of information you encounter every day and brings to your attention what it thinks is most important based on your current beliefs and focus. Sometimes, our belief system can get programmed with negative or limiting beliefs based on past experiences or messages we received growing up. But here's the good news: we can consciously reprogram our RAS with new, empowering beliefs.

How to Reprogram Your RAS:

Let's walk through the process of reprogramming your RAS:

1. First, you need to identify the limiting belief that's holding you back. Maybe it's "I'm not good enough" or "I don't deserve love."

2. Next, it's time to flip the script. Create a new, empowering belief to replace the old one.

3. Here's a powerful format to use: "In the past... Now and in the present..." This acknowledges your old belief while firmly stating your new one. It helps your brain transition more easily.

4. Add a "because" statement. This is crucial. Your belief system needs reasons to accept the new belief. The more specific and personal, the better.

5. Repetition is key. Your RAS learns through repetition. Say your new belief out loud daily, preferably while looking in a mirror to reinforce the connection with yourself.

6. Feel it in your body. As you say your new belief, really try to feel it. Emotion helps cement new neural pathways.

7. Act as if. Start behaving in ways that align with your new belief. Your actions reinforce the new programming.

Let's put this into practice. Say your limiting belief is "I'm not worthy of love unless I'm perfect." Your new, empowering belief could be "I am worthy of love exactly as I am."

Using our format, it would look like this:

"In the past, I believed I wasn't worthy of love unless I was perfect. Now and in the present, I believe I am worthy of love exactly as I am because I am a human being with inherent worth, I have unique gifts to offer the world, and my imperfections make me beautifully human."

Repeat this new belief to yourself daily, preferably while looking in the mirror. Yes, it might feel awkward at first, but stick with it. Your belief system needs repetition to accept this new programming.

As you say it, really try to feel the truth of it in your body. Maybe place a hand on your heart or visualize yourself surrounded by love.

Throughout your day, look for evidence that supports your new belief. Did someone appreciate something you did? Did you overcome a challenge? Your RAS will start to notice these things more.

Remember, this is a process. Be patient with yourself as you work to replace those old, limiting beliefs with new, empowering ones. It takes time for your belief system to fully integrate new beliefs, but with consistency and practice, you can reshape your inner narrative and cultivate deeper self-love.

Here is an example from my own work with RAS. I grew up in a home where my mother's moods were volatile. She would scream about my father and then look at me and tell me I am lazy just like him. I am not a lazy person, but for decades I believed this to be true because this belief had been coded into my RAS system.

Here is the sentence I used to replace this belief:

"In the past, I believed I was lazy based on the harsh words said by my mother when she was angry. Now and in the present, I know that I am not lazy because I consistently demonstrate drive and productivity in my daily life. I set challenging goals for myself and persistently work towards achieving them. My strong work ethic is evident in the way I approach tasks with dedication and commitment. I am constantly seeking ways to improve and grow, both personally and professionally."

Initially, the "now and in the present" statement made me uncomfortable because I had always believed that I was inherently lazy. It took some time for my mind to adjust to this new belief and let go of my old ways of thinking.

Moving Forward

Healing from the mother wound, daddy issues, and challenging sibling dynamics is a brave and powerful journey. It requires us to confront painful experiences, challenge long-held beliefs, and learn new ways of relating to ourselves and others. As ultra-independent women, this process can feel especially daunting, as we've often relied on self-sufficiency as a way to protect ourselves from further hurt.

However, by doing this inner work, cultivating supportive relationships, and consciously reprogramming our RAS, we open ourselves up to a world of connection, healing, and growth. We learn that it's okay to need others, to ask for help, and to be vulnerable in our relationships. We discover that our worth is not tied to our achievements or our ability to handle everything on our own, but rather to our inherent value as human beings.

As we've untangled the complex web of family dynamics and begun the process of reprogramming our belief system, you might be wondering how these patterns play out in our romantic lives. Well, in the next chapter, we're diving headfirst into the world of love and ultra-independence.

Remember, every step you take in understanding and healing your family dynamics, every effort to reprogram your belief system, is a step towards more fulfilling relationships in all areas of your life. You're doing important work, and I'm so proud of you for showing up for yourself in this way. Keep shining, keep growing, and keep believing in the beautiful, whole person you are becoming. Your RAS is learning to believe it too!

Inner Child Work: Meet Your Mini-Me

As we continue our journey of understanding and reprogramming our RAS, it's time to introduce you to a powerful ally: your inner child. This is that little version of you who's been hanging out in your subconscious, probably munching on imaginary cookies and waiting for someone to notice them. Working with your inner child can be a powerful tool in reprogramming your RAS to accept more nurturing beliefs about yourself.

Here's a fun exercise to get you started:

Find a photo of yourself as a child. Got it? Good. Now, imagine that little you is sitting right in front of you. What would you say to them? What do they need to hear? Maybe it's "You're enough just as you are" or "It's okay to need help sometimes." Whatever it is, say it out loud. Yes, out loud! I know it feels weird, but trust me on this one. This helps your belief system start to internalize these new, supportive messages.

Now, ask that little you what they need. Maybe it's a hug, or to be listened to, or just to play. Whatever it is, give it to them - even if it means having a dance party in your living room or building a pillow fort. Your inner child is the key to unlocking some major healing and reprogramming your RAS, so treat them like the VIP they are!

Family Constellations: A New Perspective

As we continue our journey of healing and reprogramming our RAS, let's explore another powerful tool: Family Constellations therapy. This approach can provide new insights into your family dynamics and help reprogram your RAS by giving you fresh perspectives on old patterns.

Family Constellations is almost like a game of role-playing, but instead of pretending to be fantasy characters, you're reliving your family's dynamics. Essentially, you use people or objects to represent family members and observe how they interact with each other. It's as if you're watching your own family drama unfold on a stage without the tension and discomfort of a Thanksgiving dinner.

While it's recommended to do this with a trained therapist, here's a simplified version that you can try at home:

Grab some objects to represent your family members - action figures, stuffed animals, even your fruit bowl will do. Arrange them in a way that feels right to represent your family dynamics. Now, observe. What patterns do you notice? Who's close to whom? Who's facing away? This visual representation can give you some serious "aha" moments about your family system and how it's programmed your belief system.

Forgiveness vs. Acceptance: Finding Your Path

As we delve deeper into healing our family wounds and reprogramming our RAS, it's important to address a common stumbling block: the pressure to forgive. Let's get one thing straight - forgiveness is not a mandatory pit stop on your healing journey. I repeat: You. Don't. Have. To. Forgive. Sometimes, acceptance is enough, and it's a whole lot easier to swallow. This approach can also help reprogram your RAS to focus on what you can control - your own reactions and boundaries.

Acceptance is like looking at that ugly lamp your aunt gave you and saying, "Yep, that's an ugly lamp" without feeling the need to write a sonnet about its beauty. It's acknowledging what happened without trying to sugarcoat it or make it okay.

Try this: Write down something a family member did that hurt you. Now, instead of forcing yourself to forgive, try saying, "This happened, and it wasn't okay, but I accept that I can't change the past." How does that feel? A little lighter, right? This exercise can help reprogram your belief system to stop constantly seeking resolution for past hurts.

Reparenting Techniques: Becoming Your Own Awesome Parent

As we continue our journey of healing and reprogramming our RAS, let's explore a powerful technique: reparenting. This is all about giving yourself the love, support, and guidance that you might have missed out on as a kid. It's a powerful way to reprogram your RAS with more positive, supportive messages.

Here's a reparenting exercise to try:

Next time you're facing a challenge, ask yourself, "What would a supportive parent say?" Then, say it to yourself. Out loud. With feeling! Maybe it's "You've got this!" or "It's okay to make mistakes." Whatever it is, deliver it with all the love and conviction of a parent who thinks you hang the moon. This helps reprogram your belief system to expect and internalize positive self-talk.

And hey, why stop there? Write yourself a lunch box note. Buy yourself that toy you always wanted as a kid. The goal is to lavish yourself with the kind of unconditional love and support that every child deserves. These actions can help reprogram your RAS to expect and seek out nurturing experiences.

Dealing with Resistance: When Your Family Thinks You've Joined a Cult

So, you're doing all this amazing work on yourself, setting boundaries like a boss, and communicating like a pro. But your family? They're looking at you like you've grown a second head and started speaking in tongues. This resistance is often a sign that your newly reprogrammed RAS is clashing with the old family dynamics.

Welcome to the resistance, my friend.

First things first, remember that their resistance isn't about you - it's about them. You're changing the dance steps, and they're tripping over their own feet trying to keep up. It's uncomfortable for them, and humans tend to resist discomfort like cats resist baths. Their belief system is still operating on the old family program.

Here's a handy script for when they try to push your shiny new boundaries: "I know this is different from how we've always done things, and I understand it might be uncomfortable. I'm doing this because it's important for my well-being, and ultimately, for our relationship. I hope you can respect that, even if you don't fully understand it right now." This clear communication can help reprogram both your RAS and theirs to expect and respect boundaries.

And if they still resist? Remember, you don't need their permission to take care of yourself. Keep doing your thing, keep those boundaries firm, and eventually, they'll either get on board or... well, they'll have to deal with it. Your belief system will gradually adapt to this new normal.

You've got this, you magnificent boundary-setting, self-healing, RAS-reprogramming warrior!

Exercises for Reflection and Healing:

Now, let's get practical with some exercises to help you reflect on your family dynamics, start your healing journey, and reprogram your RAS:

Exercise 1: Family Role Reflection:

Think about your family of origin. What role did you play? Were you the peacemaker, the rebel, the invisible child, the overachiever? Write down your role and how it has influenced your adult behaviors and relationships. How has this role programmed your belief system?

Exercise 2: Emotion Mapping:

Draw a simple family tree, including your parents, siblings, and grandparents. Next to each person, write down the primary emotion you associate with them. What patterns do you notice? How have these emotional associations influenced your own emotional landscape and programmed your RAS?

Exercise 3: Letter to Your Younger Self:

Write a compassionate letter to your younger self at a difficult time in your childhood. What would you say to comfort and support that child? What wisdom would you share? This exercise can help reprogram your belief system with more nurturing self-talk.

Exercise 4: Boundary Exploration:

List three situations in your family where you struggle to maintain healthy boundaries. For each situation, write down:

What boundary you'd like to set

- Why it's important to you.

- What's holding you back from setting this boundary.

- One small step you could take towards establishing this boundary.

- How might setting these boundaries help reprogram your RAS?

Exercise 5: Healing Affirmations:

Create a list of healing affirmations specific to your family wounds. For example:

"I am worthy of love and respect, regardless of my achievements."

"It's safe for me to express my needs and emotions."

"I am not responsible for other people's feelings or actions."

"I can love my family while still taking care of myself."

Use these affirmations daily to help reprogram your belief system.

Exercise 6: Gratitude and Growth:

Despite the challenges, our families often provide us with strengths and positive traits too. List three positive qualities you've developed as a result of your family experiences. How have these qualities served you in your adult life? How can you program your RAS to focus more on these strengths?

Exercise 7: Creating Your Chosen Family:

Imagine you're creating your ideal 'chosen family'.

- Who would be in it?

- What qualities would these relationships have?

- Write a description of this chosen family and how being part of it would make you feel.

- How can this vision help reprogram your belief system to seek out healthier relationships?

Remember, these exercises might bring up strong emotions. Be gentle with yourself as you work through them. It's okay to take breaks or to seek support if you need it. Each step you take is helping to reprogram your belief system for healthier patterns.

As we've untangled the complex web of family dynamics and begun the process of reprogramming our belief system, you might be wondering how these patterns play out in our romantic lives. Well, in the next chapter, we're diving headfirst into the world of love and ultra-independence.

Chapter Eight

Romance – Heart of the Brave

Her independence is fierce, but within her beats a heart brave enough to love.

Mia's Story: The Eternal Fixer

Mia wakes up with a pounding headache and a sinking feeling in her stomach. She glances at the empty space where Jake, her latest fling, was snoozing earlier. He left again without waking her or even leaving a note. As she replays the night's events, disappointment and self-doubt wash over her.

Jake, like so many men Mia gravitates towards, is emotionally unavailable and always needs fixing. Despite her better judgment, she finds herself drawn to these types, constantly seeking their approval and validation. She recognizes this pattern, rooted in her childhood, where her dad's inconsistent presence left her craving male attention and affection.

Mia's dad was the kind of guy who'd waltz in every few months with fancy presents and grandiose promises, only to disappear again without a trace. She'd wait by the window for hours, hoping to catch a glimpse of his car, her heart leaping with each false alarm. More often than not, she'd be left with a pile of unopened gifts and a hollow feeling in her chest.

Now, as an adult, Mia finds herself constantly attracted to men like her father - those who need saving, those who are always just out of reach. She pours her heart and soul into these relationships, convinced that if she just loves them enough, she can fix all their problems and make them stay.

But it never works out that way. Just like with her dad, Mia's left with empty promises and a lingering sense of inadequacy. She knows, deep down, that she deserves better, but the pull towards these emotionally unavailable men is like a magnet she can't resist.

As Mia lies in bed, staring at the ceiling, she wonders if she's doomed to repeat this pattern forever. Will she always be the one who's left behind, the one who's never quite enough? Or is there a way to break free from this cycle and find the love she truly deserves?

The Fear of Love

So here we are, my fiercely independent warrior. We've arrived at a place we've all been before, perhaps one we have promised to never tread again. Love, in all its glory or lack thereof - we're all too familiar with the pain it can bring.

For ultra-independent women like us, there's nothing more terrifying than love. We've been burned so many times that the thought of allowing ourselves to love again feels like too much to bear. From a young age, we've seen how love leaves - Dad left, Mom didn't love us enough, or we watched one of our parents grieve the loss of love. As adults, the same pattern continued - love cheated, love abused, love left us.

While many ultra-independents can be in fulfilling relationships, most of us are fearful of attachment. We don't want to get hurt, and honestly, we don't see the need for someone else in our lives. The thought of tending to another person's needs is overwhelming when our own plate is already so full.

But understanding why we feel this way is the first step towards changing our patterns. So, let's jump in and explore the roots of our fear, shall we?

The Role of Attachment Styles

Let's talk about attachment styles - think of them as your relationship blueprint. There are six main types, and understanding which one you fall into can be incredibly enlightening.

Secure: Meet Emma, a 42-year-old teacher. She's comfortable with both intimacy and independence. When her partner needs space, she doesn't panic. When she needs support, she asks for it without fear. Emma's the poster child for healthy attachment.

Anxious: Alisha, a 28-year-old graphic designer, constantly worries her boyfriend will leave her. She checks her phone obsessively for texts and feels insecure when he's out with friends. So

Avoidant: Nina, a 53-year-old lawyer, values her independence above all. She gets uncomfortable when her partner wants to spend too much time together and often pulls away when things get too intimate. This might hit close to home for many of us ultra-independents.

Fearful-Avoidant: Lila, a 29-year-old writer, craves closeness but is terrified of getting hurt. She alternates between clinging to her partner and pushing them away. It's an emotional rollercoaster, to say the least.

Anxious-Preoccupied: Mandy, a 31-year-old sales manager, needs constant reassurance in her relationships. She's always worried about her partner's feelings and often neglects her own needs.

Dismissive-Avoidant: Jenna, a 43-year-old entrepreneur, prides herself on her self-sufficiency. She rarely opens up emotionally and tends to downplay the importance of her relationships.

If you're like most ultra-independents, you might find yourself resonating with the avoidant or fearful-avoidant styles. We often choose unavailable partners – perhaps someone who lives in another town, is married, or is too busy for a real relationship. Anything that means they have to remain at arm's length, making true intimacy out of the question or we might just not date at all because we just don't think its worth the heartbreak and the hassle.

Common Relationship Patterns for Ultra-Independent Women

The Self-Protective Shield: Ultra-Independence as a Defense Against Love

As ultra-independents, we often build walls around our hearts, not just to keep others out, but to protect ourselves from the intensity of our own emotions. Let me share a personal experience that illustrates this:

I fell head over heels once in my late twenties. We were so compatible and so very similar. We would dance the night away, laugh until our stomachs hurt, and simply enjoy each other's company. I was head over heels for him, so much so that I even followed him to London for two years. The relationship was great until it wasn't. Cracks started to appear; he was lazy and seemed to bring bad luck wherever he went. Despite this, I held on because I believed our love could conquer all.

Things deteriorated, and we became more distant until it was inevitable that the relationship would come to an end. He packed his things and moved out, leaving me alone with my heartbreak and grief. The pain was excruciating. Every night, I was consumed by intense pain. My heart felt heavy and broken as I cried myself to sleep, knowing he was no longer a part of my life. The thought of never seeing or hearing from him again brought me to tears. It was like my heart was shattering into pieces that could never be put back together.

I visited him at a friend's house before he left for the US, just to say goodbye. We shared a cup of tea and then hugged and kissed before I left. As I walked down the road to catch my bus, I kept repeating to myself, "Don't look back, don't look at him because you will turn to stone." And this is what I have believed ever since, that if I love too hard, I will break again.

A few months later, while in Portugal, I met my future husband. Our love was different - I cared for him deeply but not with the same intensity as before. I knew that if he ever left me, I would be okay because I had promised myself never to let anyone hurt me like that again. My ultra-independent armor protected me from pain, or so I thought.

Many of us can relate to this feeling. We've tasted the bittersweet intensity of all-consuming love, and the shattering pain of its loss.

In response, we construct elaborate defenses:

- **Emotional distancing:** We keep our feelings in check, never allowing ourselves to fall too deeply.

- **Hyper-self-reliance:** We make sure we can handle everything on our own, so we never "need" anyone.

- **Commitment phobia:** We avoid serious relationships or sabotage them before they become too intense.

- **Perfectionism:** We set impossibly high standards for partners, ensuring no one can meet them.

- **Busyness:** We keep ourselves so occupied that we don't have time for deep emotional connections.

While these strategies may protect us from pain, they also prevent us from experiencing the full depth and beauty of love. The key is to strike a balance between self-protection and openness to love. It's certainly not an easy feat, but believe me when I say that it's worth the effort.

Limerence and Unhealthy Relationship Patterns

Let's discuss a concept that may seem unfamiliar at first - limerence. You're probably thinking, "What on earth is that?" Well, stick with me here, because this is something many of us ultra-independents fall into without even realizing it.

Limerence is an intense, often unhealthy fixation on someone who is unavailable to us. We create an elaborate fantasy relationship in our minds, and it feels so real that we might as well be writing our own romance novel. Sound familiar? Yeah, I thought it might.

We often engage in limerence because it gives us a false sense of safety. After all, how can someone break your heart if they're not actually in your life? It's almost as if our brains are saying, "Let's fall in love with that married coworker. They'll never leave their wife, so we're safe!" Sounds crazy, doesn't it?

My own experience with limerence began during my teenage years when I was being bullied at school. I would retreat to my room and daydream about the popular boy becoming my boyfriend, imagining how envious other girls would be and how much he would adore me. Fast forward to adulthood, and I was still doing the same thing - crushing on younger men or people who had explicitly told me they weren't interested.

In these fantasies, I always cast myself as the savior. It made me feel needed and important. And it served as a great distraction from any issues I didn't want to confront in my real life. Classic avoidance tactic, right?

It took me a while to figure it out, but all these limerent relationships popped up during tough times in my life. It was my brain's way of saying, "Let's focus on this imaginary love story instead of dealing with real problems!"

You may think, "What harm could come from a little daydreaming?" But trust me, limerence can spiral out of control very quickly. I've seen people sacrifice their careers for a boss they're infatuated with, all because of this illusion of love.

So how do we avoid falling into the trap of limerence? Here are my top tips:

- If someone tells you they're not interested, believe them. No ifs, ands, or buts.

- If you tend to experience limerence, be cautious with long-distance relationships. They can fuel limerent fantasies.

- If you find yourself attracted to someone who needs "fixing," ask yourself what you may be avoiding in your own life.

Remember, genuine love is not about fantasies - it's about establishing a real connection, flaws and all.

The Dark Dance of Narcissist and the Ultra-Independent

Sadly, ultra-independent women often find themselves entangled with narcissistic partners who exploit their fierce self-reliance.

You might wonder, "Why would a strong, independent woman fall for a narcissist?" Well, narcissists are like moths to our flame. They see our strength and think, "I bet I could conquer that!" And us? We see them as a challenge. It's like our kryptonite.

Let me introduce you to my client, Gabriella. She's a successful, confident entrepreneur who can handle anything that comes her way. Then along came Mark, the charming and seemingly perfect man. Initially, he treated Gabriella like the star of her own romantic movie. But over time, his kind words turned into hurtful actions.

One day, after closing a major deal at work, Gabriella was ecstatic and ready to celebrate. But when she got home, all Mark did was shrug and ask why dinner wasn't ready. This is a classic move by narcissists - they start by showering you with love and compliments, then slowly chip away at your self-esteem.

The worst part? We often stay in these toxic relationships, thinking we can change the other person if we just love them enough. But let me tell you, they won't change.

If you find yourself in a toxic dance with a narcissist, remember this: You can't change them, but you can save yourself. It's not about being strong enough to stay - it's about being strong enough to leave. Seek help, set boundaries (and stick to them!), and redirect all that energy back into yourself. Most importantly, be kind to yourself. We've all been through tough times, and staying too long in a bad situation doesn't make you weak - it makes you human.

After six more months, Gabriella finally left the relationship. During this time, we focused on rebuilding her self-esteem, and I taught her techniques to reprogram her RAS beliefs. I also encouraged her to reach out to a family member, followed by a friend. On a chilly November night while Mark was away on a business trip, she gathered her belongings, and her father came to pick her up. She hasn't seen Mark since.

Surviving a narcissistic relationship can make you stronger than ever. You learn what you will and won't tolerate in a relationship. You discover the value of your own voice and needs.

Remember, your vulnerability is not a weakness - it's your superpower. And it's something a narcissist will never truly appreciate. Use that superpower to free yourself from their grasp.

I promise, your future self will thank you for it.

"The Bad Boy Detox Program": Reprogramming Your Ultra-Independent Attraction Code

Let's talk about something many of us ultra-independent women struggle with - our attraction to "bad boys." In some cases, it may be part of Limerance where we are aware that the bad boy will never truly commit, allowing us to maintain our autonomy. Perhaps we believe we are strong enough to tame these wild spirits or that we're tough enough to handle their chaos. It's possible that this attraction stems from growing up in households where our fathers were the quintessential bad boys and our mothers took on the role of caretaker for another child.

Growing up, my bedroom walls were plastered with posters of the classic bad boy rock star. You know the type - wild, rebellious, constantly making headlines for their outrageous behavior. I was utterly infatuated with this image – the misunderstood, wild artist who needed saving. As an ultra-independent woman, I thought I could be the one to "fix" him.

For years, I found myself drawn to men like him – the troubled souls with magnetic charm. I thought my strength and independence made me capable of handling their emotional baggage. But now, in retrospect, I realize that my childhood, craving my parents' attention, had programmed me to equate love with the desperate desire for affection and the willingness to settle for breadcrumbs.

How many times have you heard yourself or a friend say, "I can handle his issues; I'm strong enough"? But the reality is, there are plenty of amazing men out there who don't need fixing; we just can't see them because our eyes are trained to laser-focus on the bad boys as soon as we enter a room.

That's where the concept of the "good guy" comes in. Think of someone who's intelligent, fun, edgy but not destructive, a gentleman, successful, faithful, and attractive. Someone who appreciates our independence rather than challenges it. I'm sure you're chuckling as you read this, thinking that this isn't the type of man you usually go for. But humor me and continue reading for a little while longer.

To reprogram my attraction code, I started by immersing myself in images of this "good guy" archetype. When I went out, I challenged myself to seek out men who embodied these characteristics. It was a difficult task; I won't deny it. At times, I found my gaze drawn back to the bad boy who had me feeling excited and fluttery inside. But I forced myself to refocus, reminding myself that changing ingrained habits takes time, determination, and consistent effort.

I kept at it, reminding myself that this was the type of man I truly wanted, listing all the reasons why he was a better choice, and acknowledging that I was no longer seeking to prove my strength by taming a wild spirit.

After months of dedicated effort (because real change takes time), I found myself at a friend's house party, suddenly realizing that three men fitting my new "good guy" ideal were sitting with me, all vying for my attention. This is a true story.

Like any new habit, I still have to catch myself sometimes, but it's getting easier. I no longer find the bad boy a turn-on. Instead, I'm excited by the reliable, funny, level-headed, quirky, and intelligent guys – the ones who complement my independence rather than test it.

Ultimately, if we ultra-independent women continue to date the red flags, nothing will change in our dating game. We have to reprogram ourselves to change what we attract, moving away from the idea that our strength is best used in "fixing" someone.

If you don't believe me, try it for yourself. Choose your ideal man, focusing on traits you haven't necessarily gone for before. Even if some of these qualities sound boring initially, give it a shot. Find photographs of people online who meet these criteria, and start training your brain to recognize and appreciate these attributes.

Challenge yourself to go out and identify three people who match your new ideal. You don't need to strike up a conversation with them right away; simply acknowledge their presence and allow yourself to feel attracted to this new type of person.

By consistently practicing the Bad Boy detox program, we'll slowly but surely reprogram our attraction code, setting ourselves up for healthier, more fulfilling relationships that complement our independence rather than challenge it.

Strategies for Healthier Relationships: Chloe's Journey

Let's look at my client Chloe and see how we collaborated to attract healthy and fulfilling romantic partners into her life. She's a corporate lawyer, successful and fiercely independent. When she first came to me, she was frustrated with her love life. She kept falling for "bad boys" who left her feeling drained and unfulfilled.

Reprogramming Attraction

We started with the "Bad Boy Detox Program." Chloe listed qualities she actually wanted in a partner - things like reliability, emotional intelligence, and kindness. No more chasing after superficial excitement. We created a vision board with images of men who possessed these traits, and it was Chloe's job to start noticing these types of men in her daily life.

Addressing Attachment Issues

Chloe had an anxious-avoidant attachment style. She craved closeness but would run away when things got too real. Together, we practiced exercises to help her feel more secure. She also began journaling about her fears and learned techniques to calm herself down when she felt like running away.

Learning Effective Communication

Expressing her needs was difficult for Chloe. Through role-playing and using "I" statements, we worked on improving her communication skills. Soon, she became comfortable saying things like, "I feel overwhelmed with work. Can we plan regular date nights to stay connected?"

Finding Balance

This was a crucial element for Chloe. We focused on balancing her need for independence with her desire for connection. She started scheduling specific "me time" while also making sure to plan activities with her partner.

Embracing Vulnerablilty

Chloe's breakthrough moment came when she opened up about a childhood inse-curity to her new partner. Instead of pushing him away when things got tough, she chose to stay and share. To her surprise, being vulnerable led to more understanding and compassion in the relationship.

Staying Present

As part of our journey together, we implemented a "no phones on date night" rule. This allowed Chloe and her partner to have quality time without digital distractions, leading to a deeper connection and genuine engagement with each other.

The Outcome

In our year working together, Chloe's entire approach to relationships had trans-formed. She began dating a man who was kind and stable. He respected her inde-pendence but also provided emotional support. Chloe learned how to effectively communicate her needs and no longer ran away from tough conversations.

Her biggest realization was that embracing vulnerability and interdependence did not mean compromising her independence. In fact, she found that these qualities only enhanced her natural strength, resulting in a more fulfilling relationship than she had ever experienced before.

Chloe's story is a testament that even the most fiercely independent women can cul-tivate healthy, well-rounded relationships without sacrificing their sense of self. It's not about changing who we are; it's about expanding our capacity for connection while staying true to ourselves.

Remember, everyone's journey is unique and takes time. Be patient with yourself, celebrate small victories, and keep moving forward. Your perfect balance of inde-pendence and connection is out there - you just need to be open to finding it.

As you work towards building healthier relationships, remember to cut yourself some slack. Change doesn't happen overnight, but every step towards more genuine connections is worth celebrating. You deserve love that respects all parts of you - your strength, vulnerability, and everything in between.

Exercises and Reflection Questions:

Exercise 1: Attachment Style Reflection

Get curious about your romantic attachment style.

- What patterns do you gravitate towards - clinging anxiously, distancing, push/pulling intimacy?

- How might these link to old survival strategies?

- Journal on ways you could update these scripts.

Exercise 2: Visualizing Secure Partnership

Visualize and describe your ideal imagery for a secure romantic partnership.

- What qualities does it embody?

- What boundaries, honoring, and freedom does it provide?

- Breathe into receiving that experience.

Exercise 3: Practicing Assertive Communication

- Practice assertive communication with "I" statements.

- Write out at least one vulnerable need or desire you'd want to express to a partner, as if speaking directly to them.

Exercise 4: De-escalation Technique

Try out a de-escalation tool the next time you feel triggered into fight/flight with your partner.

- Take some deep breaths, hug them, step outside for a break.

- Process the experience after recentering.

Exercise 5: Energy Balance Reflection

Reflect on your balance of masculine and feminine energies.

- What's abundant or deficient?

- Brainstorm small actions you could take to embody more receptivity, playfulness, intuition, or creative flow in your relationships.

Exercise 6: Interdependence Assessment

- In what ways do you currently prioritize interdependence in your relationships?

- Are there any areas where you could improve?

Exercise 7: Control and Self-Sufficiency Reflection

Think about a recent situation where you struggled with the need for control or self-sufficiency.

- How did this affect the outcome of the situation?

Exercise 8: Relationship Balance Evaluation

Take some time to reflect on your relationships.

- Do you feel that you have a good balance between independence and interdependence in your relationships?

- If not, what steps can you take to improve this balance?

The Bad Boy Detox Program:

Reprogramming Your Attraction Code

Exercise 1: Identifying Your Bad Boy

Take a moment to reflect on your dating history and the type of men you've been attracted to in the past. Write down the characteristics that define your Bad Boy - the bad boy, the misunderstood artist, the one who needs saving. Be honest with yourself and recognize the patterns in your attraction.

Worksheet 1: "My Bad Boy" traits

- Physical attributes:

- Personality traits:

- Behaviors

- Relationship dynamics:

Now that you've identified your Bad Boy, it's time to reprogram your attraction code.

Exercise 2: Finding Your Worthy Partner

Think about the qualities you truly want in a partner - the traits that will lead to a healthy, fulfilling relationship. Consider men who are intelligent, funny, reliable, and emotionally stable. These are your Worthy partners.

Worksheet 2: My Ideal Worthy Partner Traits

- Physical attributes:

- Personality traits:

- Behaviors

- Relationship dynamics:

Exercise 3: Visual Reprogramming

To begin rewiring your attraction, immerse yourself in images of men who embody your "Worthy Partner" traits. Create a Pinterest board or save images on your phone of celebrities, influencers, or even regular guys who fit this mold. Spend time each day looking at these images and training your brain to find these qualities attractive.

Exercise 4: Real-World Practice

When you're out and about, challenge yourself to spot at least three people who match your new Worthy Partner ideal. Don't focus on the bad boys who usually catch your eye. Instead, give your attention to the guys who might have flown under your radar before. Smile at them, make eye contact, and strike up a conversation if you feel comfortable.

Remember, reprogramming your attraction code takes time and patience. You might find yourself slipping back into old patterns, but don't beat yourself up. Gently redirect your focus and keep practicing. Over time, you'll find yourself naturally drawn to the "good guys" of the world - the men who are ready for a real, healthy relationship.

Worksheet 3: My Reprogramming Journey

- Bad Boy moments (when I found myself attracted to the wrong type).

- Worthy Partner moments (when I successfully redirected my attraction).

- Progress and self-reflection.

By following the Bad Boy Detox Program and completing these exercises and worksheets, you'll be well on your way to attracting the right kind of man and building the relationship you truly deserve.

Now that we've navigated the choppy waters of romantic relationships, let's turn our attention to another crucial aspect of our lives - friendships. In the next chapter, we'll explore how ultra-independence shapes our platonic connections and learn how to build deeper, more fulfilling friendships without losing ourselves in the process.

Chapter Nine

Friendships

A friend is someone who knows the song in your heart and can sing it back to you when you have forgotten the words.

Sarah's Story: The Loneliest Number

Sarah's fingers hover over her phone screen, a text message half-composed. "Hey, want to grab coffee this weekend?" She stares at the words, her thumb poised over the send button. With a sigh, she deletes the message and tosses her phone onto the couch.

"What's the point?" she mutters, running a hand through her hair. "She's probably busy anyway."

Sarah glances around her immaculate apartment, everything in its place, just as she likes it. The silence, usually a comfort, feels oppressive tonight. She walks to the window, watching the bustling street below. Couples stroll hand in hand, groups of friends spill out of restaurants, their laughter floating up to her like a distant melody.

Her reflection stares back at her: successful career woman on the outside, lonely soul on the inside. Sarah turns away, unable to bear the contrast between her isolated perch and the vibrant life below.

She thinks about Megan from work, always inviting her to happy hours that Sarah invariably declines. "I've got a deadline," she'll say, or "I'm not feeling well." Excuses that grow more elaborate with each invitation.

The truth is, Sarah is terrified. Terrified of letting people in, of depending on anyone but herself. The memory of her best friend's betrayal in high school still stings, a wound that never quite healed.

"I'm fine on my own," Sarah whispers, a mantra she's repeated countless times. But tonight, the words taste bitter.

She walks to her home office, intending to lose herself in work as she always does. But instead of reaching for her laptop, she finds herself opening the bottom drawer of her desk. There, buried under a stack of files, is a photo album she hasn't looked at in years.

Sarah's fingers tremble as she opens it. Pictures of happier times stare back at her - Sarah and her friends at prom, laughing at a sleepover, hugging on graduation day. When had she started pushing everyone away?

A lump forms in her throat. She slams the album shut, shoving it back into the drawer.

Friendships and Our Lone Island

We ultra-independents prefer to keep our circles small. It's less complicated, safer, and aligns with our solitary nature. But let's face it - this tendency didn't develop out of thin air. Our experiences have taught us that opening up to others can often lead to disappointment.

Forming friendships has never been my strong suit. As a child, I watched others effortlessly making connections while I stood by, wondering what their secret was. So I stuck to one-on-one friendships; fewer people meant fewer complications for me.

My primary school experience was mostly positive until I turned 12. That's when a 13-year-old girl appeared, with her bleached hair and rebellious nature. She was the type to smoke behind the school shed, adding an edge to her cool persona. Now, in retrospect, I understand that her tumultuous home life greatly impacted her actions. Unfortunately, her personal issues often spilled over into our friend group and caused unnecessary drama.

Secondary school? That was a whole new level of challenge. Our little primary school group, along with Miss Drama Queen, got thrown into this massive new school. Desperate to fit in with the popular kids, I changed myself to please them - but it only backfired at 14 when they turned on me. They would surround me during breaks and hurl insults while the teachers turned a blind eye.

School became my personal nightmare. Not only did I have no friends, but I was also terrified of the constant bullying. It spread everywhere, following me into classrooms and hallways. They fixated on my weight - yes, I was chubby, but not exactly obese. But why let facts get in the way of a good insult, right?

When my parents brought the issue to the deputy head, his solution was for me to leave the school instead of addressing the bullies themselves. This experience shattered my belief in justice and support.

All of this shaped my perception of friendships: they required constant effort, were full of potential betrayal, and you had to keep pleasing people or risk being cast aside. The worst part? Realizing that no one was going to stand up for me. I was alone.

The bullying eventually stopped when they moved on to another victim, but the damage was done. My approach to relationships had been permanently altered.

Fast forward to 28-year-old me in London. I found myself in this group of friends connected to a guy I was head over heels for. They were toxic and mean, constantly gossiping about those not present. Despite knowing they were not good for me, I desperately wanted their acceptance. For two years, I tried to mold myself to fit into their world, all because I craved their approval.

This experience was the final cherry on top of my belief about friendships and my fear of them. It reinforced everything I had learned from my past: that friendships were risky, that I had to change myself to be accepted, and that even then, I could be discarded or hurt at any moment.

These cumulative experiences shaped my approach to relationships profoundly. They programmed my mind to be hyper-vigilant about potential rejection or betrayal in social situations. As a result, I retreated further into my ultra-independence, convincing myself that I was better off alone.

For many of us, our minds are programmed to believe that connections are fleeting. People leave - through death, betrayal, or simply drifting apart. Yet, deep down, we know these bonds are vital. We all need a friend, even as we struggle to work our way through the complexities of letting others in.

It's a challenging journey, this friendship business. But perhaps it's worth another attempt. After all, what's the alternative? A lifetime of isolation? Maybe it's time to start rewriting our friendship stories, one careful step at a time.

Spotting the Friendship Red Flags

As strong, independent women, we're used to handling our own affairs without leaning on others. But let's be honest - this self-reliance can sometimes leave us blind to toxic friendships lurking in our lives. It's crucial to recognize when a friendship has gone from sweet to sour. So, what are the telltale signs we need to watch out for?

Here are some major red flags that should set off our internal alarms:

Constant Criticism:

If your friend's idea of conversation is a non-stop critique of your life choices, appearance, or achievements, that's not okay. A true friend builds you up, not tears you down.

Lack of Reciprocity:

Friendship is a two-way street, not a one-way expressway. If you're always there for them, ready with a listening ear or a helping hand, but they're mysteriously MIA when you need support, that's a problem.

Disrespect for Boundaries:

A good friend respects your limits and your need for space. If they're constantly pushing your boundaries, showing up uninvited, or pressuring you to do things you're not comfortable with, it's time to have a serious chat.

Emotional Drainage:

Do you find yourself dreading hanging out with them? Feel like you need a week-long nap after every interaction? That's your gut telling you something's off. Friendships should energize you, not leave you feeling like you've run an emotional marathon.

Gossip and Betrayal:

If your friend's favorite pastime is talking about others behind their backs, chances are you're starring in similar conversations when you're not around. A trustworthy friend doesn't turn your confidences into tomorrow's hot gossip.

Competitive Behavior:

Life isn't a race, and friendship certainly shouldn't feel like one. If your friend is always trying to one-up you - be it in career, relationships, or personal achievements - that's not healthy companionship, it's a rivalry.

Lack of Trust:

Trust is the bedrock of any solid friendship. If you find yourself hesitating to share your secrets or vulnerabilities with your friend, it's worth examining why. Do they have a history of betraying your trust? Or do you simply not feel safe opening up to them?

Conditional Support:

A true friend stands by you through thick and thin, not just when it's convenient or beneficial for them. If their support comes with strings attached or disappears when you're going through a rough patch, that's not genuine friendship.

Remember, it's okay to let go of friendships that are dragging you down. Ending a toxic friendship doesn't make you a bad person or a friendship failure. In fact, it's a sign that you're growing, evolving, and prioritizing your well-being. It takes strength to recognize when a relationship is no longer serving you and even more courage to walk away.

Trust your gut on this one. We independent women have finely-tuned instincts - it's time we start listening to them when it comes to our friendships too. After all, we deserve relationships that add value to our lives, not drain it.

So, take a good, hard look at your friendships. Are they lifting you up or weighing you down? It's time to nurture the relationships that help you thrive and let go of those that hold you back.

Navigating the Digital Friendship Maze

The relationship between social media and our friendships is complex. On one hand, it's a powerful tool that allows us to stay connected with our friends, sharing moments of our lives and sending quick messages no matter the time of day. However, on the other hand, it can also be a source of comparison, anxiety, and feelings of inadequacy as we constantly compare ourselves to others on these platforms.

Here are some tips for maintaining healthy digital friendships:

Focus on Quality, Not Quantity: The number of friends you have on social media doesn't matter as much as the quality of those relationships.

Establish Limits: It's perfectly acceptable to mute or unfollow individuals whose content brings negativity to your social media feed. And no, you are not obligated to respond to every message immediately. You can be logged in but not actively engaged in a text conversation.

Be Authentic: Share your real self, not just the highlight reel.

Use It as a Tool, Not a Replacement: Social media should enhance your friendships, not replace face-to-face interactions.

Mindful Consumption: Be aware of how much time you're spending on social media and how it makes you feel.

How often have you found yourself staring at a message, trying to figure out if your friend is truly angry or simply preoccupied? It's like attempting to decipher emotions through a solid barrier. That's why I always advise my clients: if it's important, make a phone call or arrange a video chat. Believe me, it'll prevent unnecessary overthinking and potential conflicts.

Remember, though, online friendships are just one piece of the puzzle. They're great for keeping in touch, but they shouldn't replace good old-fashioned face-to-face time. So make an effort to balance your digital chats with real-world meetups. Even if it's just grabbing a quick coffee, it'll do wonders for your friendships.

Building Healthier Friendships: Anya's Story

Anya is a marketing executive, fiercely independent, and struggling with friendships. When she first came to me, she was feeling isolated and unsure how to build meaningful connections without compromising her independence.

Anya's story might sound familiar to you. She'd been burned by friendships in the past, leaving her wary of getting close to people. Her calendar was packed with work commitments, but her social life was practically non-existent. She'd convinced herself she was fine on her own, but deep down, she longed for genuine connections.

Here's how we worked together to help Anya build healthier friendships:

Identifying Her Friendship Style

First, we dug into Anya's past experiences with friends. We uncovered a pattern of attracting high-drama individuals who often left her feeling drained. Anya realized she'd been subconsciously recreating the chaotic friendships she'd experienced in her youth.

Tool: Friendship Pattern Recognition

- We created a "friendship timeline," mapping out Anya's significant friendships from childhood to present.

- For each friendship, we noted the dynamics, emotions, and outcomes.

This visual representation helped Anya see recurring patterns in her friendships.

Setting Friendship Boundaries

We worked on establishing clear boundaries. Anya practiced saying no to social obligations that didn't align with her values or energy levels. She started communicating her needs more clearly, telling friends when she needed alone time without feeling guilty.

Tool: The Boundary Blueprint

We developed a personalized "Boundary Blueprint" for Anya.

- This included her non-negotiables in friendships (e.g., respect for her time, no drama).

- We also created scripts for assertively communicating these boundaries.

Quality Over Quantity

Instead of trying to build a large social circle, we focused on cultivating a few meaningful friendships. Anya identified two potential friends who shared her interests and values. She made an effort to deepen these relationships through regular, quality interactions.

Tool: The Friendship Focus Plan

We created a "Friendship Focus Plan" targeting 2-3 potential close friends.

- This plan included shared interests, planned activities, and communication goals.

- We set realistic expectations for the pace of deepening these friendships.

Balancing Independence and Connection

Anya learned to schedule "friend time" into her week, just like she would a work meeting. This helped her maintain her independence while also nurturing her friendships. She found that having set times for socializing actually made her feel more in control.

Tool: The Independence-Connection Calendar

We designed a weekly schedule that balanced alone time, work time, and friend time.

- This visual tool helped Anya see that friendships didn't have to overwhelm her schedule.

- We included buffer time before and after social interactions for Anya to recharge.

Vulnerability Practice

This was tough for Anya. We started small, with her sharing minor concerns or hopes with her closest friend. As she saw that being vulnerable didn't lead to judgment or rejection, she gradually opened up more.

Tool: The Vulnerability Ladder

We created a "Vulnerability Ladder" with steps from least to most vulnerable.

- Anya started at the bottom (e.g., sharing a mild frustration about work) and gradually climbed up.

- Each successful share built her confidence in being more open.

We will discuss this more in the chapter on Vulnerability.

Redefining Friendship Expectations

Anya had to let go of the idea that friends should be available 24/7 or that friendships should be effortless. We worked on accepting that good friendships require effort and understanding, but shouldn't be a constant source of stress.

Tool: The Friendship Reality Check

We listed Anya's current beliefs about friendship and examined their validity.

- For each unrealistic expectation, we crafted a more balanced, healthy alternative.

- This became a reference guide for Anya when she felt old beliefs creeping in.

The Results

During our time working together, Anya formed two close friendships, which was a major breakthrough for her. Trust and vulnerability were still areas she struggled with, but she had made significant strides.

Most importantly, Anya discovered that true friendship doesn't weaken her independence – it enhances it. She found that having supportive friends actually made her feel more confident in her self-reliance, knowing she had a safety net if she ever needed it.

Moving Forward

Building and maintaining friendships when you're fiercely independent isn't always easy. It takes time, effort, and a bit of courage to open up and let people in.

Be patient with yourself. Celebrate the small wins, like reaching out to a friend you haven't talked to in a while or opening up about something personal. Your ability to connect and be vulnerable? That's not a weakness. It's a superpower.

As you work on your friendships, you might find something surprising. Your independence isn't threatened by having close friends. If anything, it's enhanced. Having people who support you, understand you, and appreciate your quirks can actually make you feel more secure in your independence.

So go on, give it a shot. Your future self (and your future friends) will thank you for it.

Exercises and Worksheets

Exercise 1: Friendship Inventory

Make a list of your current friendships. For each one, answer the following questions:

- How does this friendship make me feel?

- What do I appreciate about this person?

- What challenges do I face in this friendship?

- How can I deepen this connection?

Exercise 2: Vulnerability Challenge

Choose one friend and challenge yourself to share something personal that you normally wouldn't. It could be a fear, a hope, or a struggle you're facing. Afterward, reflect on:

- How did it feel to open up?

- How did your friend respond?

- What did you learn from this experience?

Exercise 3: Friendship Values Worksheet

Identify your top 5 values in friendship (e.g., trust, honesty, loyalty, fun, intellectual stimulation). For each value, write:

- Why is this important to me?

- How can I embody this value in my friendships?

- How can I communicate this need to my friends?

Exercise 4: Boundary-Setting Practice

Think of a situation where you need to set a boundary with a friend. Write out:

- What is the issue?

- How does it make you feel?

- What boundary do you need to set?

- How can you communicate this boundary clearly and kindly?

Exercise 5: Gratitude Journal

For one week, write down three things you appreciate about your friends each day. At the end of the week, reflect on how this practice has impacted your perspective on friendship.

Exercise 6: Friendship Action Plan

Choose one friendship you'd like to nurture. Create an action plan with specific steps you'll take to invest in this relationship over the next month. This could include:

- Scheduling regular catch-ups

- Planning a fun activity together

- Finding ways to support your friend's goals or interests

Exercise 7: Friendship Vision Board

Create a vision board (physical or digital) of your ideal friendships. Include images and words that represent the qualities you want in your friendships, the activities you'd like to share, and how you want to feel in these relationships. This visual representation can help clarify your friendship goals and motivate you to take action.

Remember, you are worthy of connection, of laughter-filled evenings, of deep conversations, of having someone to call when life gets tough. You are worthy of friendship in all its messy, beautiful glory. So go out there and create the connections your heart has been longing for. I'm rooting for you every step of the way.

We've seen how ultra-independence impacts our personal relationships, but what about our professional lives? In the next chapter, we'll step into the office and examine how our self-reliant tendencies play out in the workplace. Get ready to discover new ways to thrive professionally while fostering healthy interdependence with colleagues.

Chapter Ten

The Workplace

Success is not measured by the heights of our solitary achievements but by the depth of our collaborative efforts.

Linda's Story: The Invulnerable Executive

It's eleven PM, and Linda's fingers dance frantically across her laptop keyboard. The office is so quiet you could hear a pin drop, but her eyes are glued to the screen, scanning quarterly sales reports as if her life depends on it. She reaches for her coffee mug, wincing as the cold, bitter liquid hits her tongue. Fourth cup tonight, but who's counting?

A notification pops up—another email from Chuck. Linda's stomach flips before she opens it. "Hey ladies, don't forget your pink hard hats for tomorrow's site visit!" She deletes it without responding, jaw clenching.

Catching her reflection in the darkened window, Linda takes stock. Crisp white shirt? Check. Hair still immaculate? Double-check. Not a hint of the bone-deep exhaustion she feels. Good. Can't show any cracks when you're the only woman on the senior leadership team.

Her mind wanders to this morning's executive meeting. She can still hear Steve's voice drowning out her carefully prepared cost-saving proposals. She'd spoken up, voice firm and assertive, but it was like she was invisible. That familiar sting of dismissal burns in her chest.

Linda shakes it off. No time for self-pity. She learned long ago that emotions were a luxury she couldn't afford in this cutthroat corporate world.

Her eyes fall on the framed photo on her desk—her younger self, fresh-faced and eager, receiving an award at her first internship. She remembers the "congratulatory" pats that lingered too long, the leering smiles that made her skin crawl. That naive girl is long gone, replaced by a woman who knows how to play the game.

In a few hours, she'll get a little sleep, shower, and slip on her power suit—her armor against the world. She'll stride into the morning meeting, her face a mask of cool confidence. She'll shut down interruptions with hard data and unwavering assertiveness.

Because that's what it takes to survive in this world. To be invulnerable. To be utterly, completely independent.

Balancing Ambition and Well-being in the Workplace

As highly independent woman, we shine at work but also face unique challenges. Our self-reliance and drive make us great employees. We aim high, climb the career ladder, and earn praise for our hard work.

But our independence can cause problems too. We often don't like asking for help, even with small tasks. This can leave us feeling tired and alone. We push ourselves too hard without realizing it, taking on more work than we should.

We often feel most comfortable at work because it's based on our skills and effort, not emotions. This feeling of control can be misleading though. We might not notice we're burning out as we keep pushing forward, driven by our need to survive and keep our jobs.

Our determination and work ethic make us valuable team members. However, these traits can also make us forget about the importance of balance and taking care of ourselves. As we build our careers, it's important to recognize both the good and bad sides of being so independent at work.

I once worked so hard at a corporate job that when the IT manager left, they didn't replace him for six whole months. There I was, heavily pregnant, running the IT department for a quarter of the salary. Did I complain? Nope. I was like a hamster on a wheel, believing they'd notice my worth and reward me, that I was just proving myself. I didn't know how to say no or ask for what I wanted because heaven forbid I upset anyone. So I just did it, right up to two weeks before giving birth.

The day after my son was born, there I was in the hospital bed, laptop perched on my lap. But that's when my body said, "Enough is enough," and a duodenal ulcer burst, landing me in emergency surgery.

The company sent flowers (how thoughtful), and when I returned after five months of healing, my desk had been moved to a small room far away from the team, and all my projects were given away.

The moral of the story? They can replace you in a heartbeat, folks.

High Functioning Anxiety in the Workplace

Let's talk about high functioning anxiety in the workplace. This is something I see all too often with my ultra-independent clients. High-functioning anxiety can manifest as perfectionism, overworking, and an inability to relax or delegate tasks. While it may seem like these traits lead to success, they often come at a significant cost to our mental and physical well-being.

Emma, my client, worked her way up the corporate ladder in a retail company, starting in the buying department. Twenty-six years later, she runs the sourcing department and is part of the executive team. Growing up in a single-mother household where her father left when she was young, Emma watched her mom succeed on her own and promised herself she could do the same - and even better.

When you see Emma, she's always put together - clothes perfect, makeup precise. Her home is immaculate, and her children are always on their best behavior. But in our weekly sessions, she confides that keeping up this appearance is incredibly difficult. She's terrified people might realize she's not in control all the time.

Emma judges her accomplishments in life based on her career because it's been the area she can control. She's had two marriages and is now single, struggling to meet anyone because she doesn't let her emotions intervene. It's very difficult for partners because they never get to see the true Emma, only the version she portrays.

Here's how we worked together to help Emma manage her high-functioning anxiety and find more balance:

Perfectionism Detox:

To break her perfectionistic habits, Emma and I began with small steps. She intentionally left the house with a slightly disheveled hairstyle or sent an email without checking it multiple times. For someone like Emma, this was a challenge, so we documented her feelings in a journal as she let go of her need to be perfect in these minor instances.

Emotion Check-Ins:

Emma set alarms on her phone to go off three times a day. When they did, she'd take a moment to identify what she was feeling. This helped build her emotional awareness and made it easier to connect with others authentically.

The "Good Enough" List:

We created a list of five areas in Emma's life where she typically strived for perfection. Next to each, we wrote what "good enough" would look like. For example, instead of "My house must always be spotless," we wrote "My house is clean enough to be healthy and tidy enough to be comfortable."

Vulnerability Challenge:

Once a week, Emma shared something personal or slightly vulnerable with a trusted colleague or friend. It didn't have to be deep dark secrets - even sharing that she was nervous about a presentation or having a tough day helped build authentic connections.

Remember, balance isn't about perfectly dividing your time between work and personal life. It's about creating a life that feels fulfilling and authentic to you. As you work on letting go of high-functioning anxiety, be patient with yourself. Change takes time, but every small step towards authenticity and self-compassion is a victory.

Recognizing Toxic Work Cultures

While our inner drive shapes our work experience, outside factors can greatly affect how we feel. One of the biggest issues is toxic workplaces. We've all encountered them - places where you wake up feeling sick to your stomach, dreading the day ahead.

The main sign of these unhealthy work cultures is often the infamous "Asshole Boss." It's a common experience, almost like a rite of passage in the working world. From childhood, we're taught to put up with bad treatment, just like we did with bullies in school. We're told that having a job is a privilege, one that apparently comes with the cost of enduring abuse from higher-ups.

As highly independent people, we often make this situation worse. We tell ourselves, "I'm tougher than any bully. I can handle whatever they throw at me." So we keep going, day after day. But the negative atmosphere doesn't stay at the office - it follows us home, casting a shadow over our personal lives.

The constant flood of negativity - being told we're not good enough, living in fear of consequences, walking on eggshells, watching our boss's mood swings - takes a huge toll. It seeps into every interaction, affecting how we see ourselves and the world around us.

Interestingly, many of my clients report a repeat pattern of ending up with toxic bosses. This isn't by chance. We often get stuck in these unhealthy patterns because they've become familiar. Strangely, a calm, respectful work environment might feel unsettling - we've become so used to stress and drama that we don't know how to function without it.

Spotting these unhealthy patterns is the first step towards breaking free from them. It's crucial to understand that putting up with abuse is not necessary for success at work. In fact, it often holds us back from growing and feeling good.

So, what exactly defines an asshole boss? Let me break it down for you:

- Their attitude is consistently negative, with a constant stream of criticism towards any and every aspect.

- They do not value your personal time and are never satisfied, no matter how much effort you put in.

- It seems impossible for them to find anything positive to discuss.

- They resort to bullying tactics and constantly belittle and intimidate others.

- Their narrow-minded outlook leads them to view all employees as either incompetent or worthless.

- Additionally, they manipulate situations and create strife between coworkers.

Asshole bosses often create a dynamic of "scapegoats" and "golden children" in the office. The golden child gets showered with praise and attention... until they don't. Because eventually, they'll fall from grace and possibly become the new scapegoat. Meanwhile, the scapegoat can never do anything right, no matter how hard they try.

This toxic work environment only strengthens our ultra-independent armor. We put up more walls, feeling unsafe and unable to trust, just like we might have felt in childhood. But just because we can handle it, doesn't mean we should. It's exhausting, unhealthy, and affects every aspect of our lives, including our personal relationships and future career choices.

Now, let's explore how we cope with stress in these circumstances:

Fight: This leads to constant conflict with the boss. You think you're asserting dominance and standing your ground, but really it's a never-ending battle leading to your burnout, not theirs.

Freeze: You agree to work longer, harder hours on the hamster wheel of your boss's demands. You believe you can't leave because no one else would hire you. This sad, limiting option restrains your true potential.

Fawn: The people-pleaser takes over. You'll work early, late, answering emails at night, volunteering for more work - anything to earn crumbs of praise and validation from your boss, who is amused to see you grovel. It feels like control, but you'll never be good enough in their eyes.

Flight: This is the response I advocate. Get out of there as soon as possible, like warning a child away from a hot stove. Staying tells your soul it's okay to be treated this way, and you're ultimately harming yourself.

But how can you leave if you don't have another job ready?

Here's the answer:

It's important to take a break, even if it's just a few days off work. This will give you time to relax and let go of any built-up stress from your job. Once you feel rested and refreshed, start thinking about your choices. You may be surprised at the new ideas that come to mind now that you've allowed yourself to think about leaving your current situation.

I understand how hard it can be to decide to leave when you feel stuck and tired from all the bad treatment. However, always remember that you deserve better. You should be valued and treated with kindness and respect. It's not about how good you are or what you've achieved; it's about how little they care about you. They are the ones who need to change.

Use your ultra independence as a power here to push yourself into positive change, out of this unhealthy environment. Believe in yourself enough to get away from the mean boss.

Maybe you've already left that job, but the memory still stays in your mind, making you very alert to possible warning signs in new workplaces. The past bad treatment has left deep emotional hurts. But don't let yourself think that any of this was your fault. You deserve to be treated with respect, care, and appreciation for your hard work. It's not wrong to have high standards for yourself and to want good things in life. No matter how hard you try, you will never earn the respect of a mean boss because they simply don't value you as a person.

Remember, you're not alone in this. Many of us have been there, and we've found our way out. You can too. Your strong independence is a strength - use it to stand up for yourself, to know your worth, and to create the good work environment you deserve. You can do this!

Mental Health and the Workplace

While unhealthy work cultures can badly affect mental health, there's a growing understanding of the importance of mental well-being at work. In recent years, we've seen a positive change in how companies view mental health; things are starting to get better.

For too long, we've been told to hide our feelings, push through the hard times, and just be glad we have a job. The harmful effects of this way of thinking on people have been serious. We are not machines; we are human beings, and it's time that is recognized and respected.

My client, Sabrina, works as a project manager in a fast-moving tech company. She saw her team was struggling with being overworked and stressed, which was affecting their work and overall happiness. Instead of ignoring the problem or pushing her team to "toughen up," Sabrina decided to start regular mental health check-ins.

She began with simple, unnamed surveys asking team members about their stress levels, work-life balance, and any problems they were facing. Then, she introduced optional weekly "wellness walks" where team members could take a thirty-minute break to walk and talk with coworkers.

The results were amazing. Not only did team spirit improve, but work output actually increased. People felt seen and valued, which made them more committed to their work. Plus, the better communication helped find and solve problems more quickly.

Navigating Gender Dynamics

Now, let's talk about something we can't ignore - being a woman in the workplace, especially an ultra-independent one. It adds another dimension to our professional experiences, doesn't it?

We've been discussing various workplace challenges, but gender dynamics deserve special attention. They can complicate things in ways that aren't always obvious at first glance.

I've been there, and I'm guessing many of you have too. It's not just about the obvious barriers; it's also about the subtle interactions, the unspoken expectations, and the unique pressures we face.

I spent twenty years in the technology industry, a mainly male-dominated field with very few women. Early on, I was berated for being "too emotional, too much of a girl." I quickly learned to be one of the boys because if I was going to succeed in this industry, I needed to behave like them. I would laugh at their misogynistic jokes, hide my emotions, and act more stoic.

As my career grew and I found myself as the only woman on the leadership team of a medium-sized tech company, I began to dread going to the office each morning. Putting on a mask of toughness and manliness was tiring, and by the time I got home, I was drained. But even in my personal life, I couldn't just shake off that version of myself. The dismissive and unemotional persona stayed, affecting my relationships, how I saw myself, and my overall well-being. This pressure to fit in follows us beyond work, seeping into every part of our lives. We get so used to hiding our emotions and changing to survive that we lose touch with our true selves. Under all these layers of adaptation, we may find ourselves wondering who we really are.

However, I've come to understand this: our femininity, emotions, and unique views as women are not flaws to be hidden. They are strengths that, when embraced, can lead to remarkable creativity, caring leadership, and a more balanced and effective work environment.

So, how did I start to reclaim my authentic self in this male-dominated industry? Well, it wasn't about swinging to the other extreme and rejecting all traditionally masculine traits. It was about finding a balance that felt true to me, that allowed me to bring my whole self to work.

First things first, I sought out my tribe. I started connecting with other women in tech, both in my company and through industry events. We formed a small networking group, and I have to say, having that kind of support made all the difference. It was like discovering an oasis in the midst of a desert - suddenly, I didn't feel so isolated anymore.

Then, I decided to become the mentor I wish I'd had early in my career. I reached out to younger women in the company, offering guidance and support. Funnily enough, this ended up being a two-way street. Their fresh perspectives and enthusiasm reminded me why I fell in love with tech in the first place.

As I gained more influence in the company, I started pushing for more inclusive policies. I advocated for things like flexible working hours and diversity in hiring. It wasn't always easy, but every small win felt like a victory for all of us.

One of the biggest changes I made was embracing my own way of leading. Instead of trying to copy the guys' tough-talk approach, I focused on my strengths as a woman. I found that my ability to show understanding, and develop teamwork were actually very valuable leadership skills. I started to use my instincts more, trusting my gut feelings about people and situations. I wasn't afraid to show my human side when it fit, which surprisingly created a more open and creative team environment. My natural ability to multi task and see the big picture while managing details turned out to be a huge plus in managing projects. Who knew that using these typically feminine qualities could be so powerful in the boardroom?

And finally, I learned to set boundaries. No more laughing at inappropriate jokes or staying for after-work drinks when I didn't want to. I realized I didn't have to be "one of the boys" to be respected and successful. In fact, being authentically myself earned me more respect in the long run.

It wasn't an overnight transformation, and there were definitely bumps along the way. But by being true to myself, I wasn't just advancing my own career - I was changing the landscape for all the women who would come after me. And let me tell you, that feels pretty damn good.

Workplace Survival Toolkit

Now that we've explored various workplace challenges, from high-functioning anxiety to toxic cultures and gender dynamics, let's equip you with some practical tools to navigate these issues. Think of this as your survival kit for the corporate jungle:

Set Clear Boundaries:

Learn to say no to unreasonable requests. Practice phrases like, "I'd love to help, but my plate is full right now. Can we reassess my workload?" It might feel uncomfortable at first, but it's essential for maintaining your sanity and productivity.

Schedule Self-Care:

Block out time in your calendar for breaks, exercise, or meditation. Treat these appointments as non-negotiable. Remember, you can't pour from an empty cup.

Build a Support Network:

Cultivate relationships with colleagues who uplift and support you. Consider finding a mentor or joining a professional women's group. Having allies at work can make all the difference when facing challenges.

Document Everything:

Keep a record of your achievements, positive feedback, and any incidents of unfair treatment. This can be invaluable for performance reviews or if you need to report toxic behavior.

Practice Assertive Communication:

Use "I" statements to express your needs and concerns. For example, "I feel overwhelmed when I'm given last-minute assignments. I'd appreciate more notice in the future." This approach is clear and professional without being confrontational.

Know Your Worth:

Regularly research industry standards for your position. Be prepared to negotiate for fair compensation and treatment. Remember, you're not asking for a favor - you're advocating for what you deserve.

Create an Exit Strategy:

Always have an updated resume and a savings fund. This gives you the freedom to leave a toxic environment if necessary. Knowing you have options can be incredibly empowering.

Delegate, Delegate, Delegate:

I cannot emphasize this enough. You do not have to do everything yourself. Trust others to do the work, or even trust them to get it wrong and learn from it. Let go of carrying everything on your shoulders. This is crucial for your well-being and for developing your team.

Embrace Your Femininity:

Be a woman and be proud of it. There's no need to behave like a man – the workplace is for all of us. Your unique perspective and approach as a woman are valuable assets. Don't shy away from qualities often associated with femininity, such as empathy, intuition, or collaborative leadership styles.

Remember, your ultra-independence is a strength, but it doesn't mean you have to do everything alone. It's okay to ask for help, to take breaks, and to prioritize your well-being. You're not just a worker - you're a whole person with needs, desires, and a life outside of work. Honor that, and you'll find yourself not just surviving, but thriving in your career.

Final Thoughts

As we wrap up this chapter, I want you to remember something crucial: You are more than your job. Your worth isn't defined by your productivity, your title, or how many hours you put in at the office. You are a complex, multifaceted human being with intrinsic value that exists outside of what you can produce or achieve.

As ultra-independent women, we have unique strengths that make us valuable assets in any workplace. Our drive, our resilience, our ability to take on challenges - these are superpowers. But like any superpower, they need to be used wisely and in balance with self-care and connection.

Whatever it means for you, I want you to know that you have permission to prioritize your own well-being. You have permission to be imperfect, to make mistakes, to have off days. You have permission to be human.

You've got this, and I'm rooting for you every step of the way.

Exercises and Reflection Questions:

Exercise 1: Work-Life Balance Assessment:

Take a moment to assess your work-life balance.

- On a scale of one to ten, how satisfied are you with your current balance

- What's one small step you could take this week to improve it?

Exercise 2: Mental Health Check-In:

Rate the following statements on a scale of one (strongly disagree) to five (strongly agree):

- I feel comfortable discussing mental health concerns with my supervisor.

- My workplace provides resources for mental health support.

- I feel able to take mental health days when needed without guilt.

- My workload feels manageable most of the time.

- I have a good work-life balance.

Now, reflect on your answers. Are there areas where you'd like to see improvement? What's one small step you could take to prioritize your mental health at work?

Exercise 3: Gender Dynamics Reflection:

- Have you ever felt pressured to conform to masculine norms in the workplace?

- How did it affect you both professionally and personally?

Exercise 4: Toxic Work Environment Reflection:

- Think about a time when you experienced a toxic work environment. How did you respond?

- Which of the stress responses (fight, freeze, fawn, flight) did you default to?

- How might you approach a similar situation differently now, armed with this new understanding?

Exercise 5: Workplace Boundaries Exercise:

Identify three boundaries you'd like to set or strengthen in your workplace. For each boundary, write down:

- What the boundary is?

- Why it's important to you?

- How you'll communicate this boundary?

- Potential challenges in maintaining this boundary?

- Strategies to overcome these challenges.

Exercise 6: Self-Care Action Plan:

Create a weekly self-care action plan for your work life. Include at least one activity for each workday that nurtures your well-being. This could be as simple as a ten-minute meditation during lunch or a quick walk around the block between meetings.

Exercise 7: Professional Development Vision Board:

Create a vision board (physical or digital) that represents your ideal professional life. Include images and words that represent your career goals, work environment, and how you want to feel in your job. Use this as a tool to guide your career decisions and remind yourself of your professional aspirations.

Remember, these exercises are meant to help you reflect, grow, and take action towards a more fulfilling professional life. Be patient with yourself as you work through them, and celebrate each small step you take towards creating a work life that honors your whole self.

As we've explored the professional realm, you might have noticed a common thread - the need for emotional awareness and openness. In the next chapter, we're going to dive deep into the often scary, always rewarding world of vulnerability and emotional intelligence. Prepare to unlock new levels of self-understanding and connection.

Chapter Eleven

Vulnerability and Trust

Love is not a surrender of independence, but a celebration of the courage to be vulnerable and the wisdom to rely on another.

Tamzin's Story: The Stoic Surgeon

The operating room goes quiet as Tamzin finishes the last stitch. Six hours of intense focus, with a life at stake, are over. She steps back from the table, her shoulders drooping slightly under her heavy surgical gown.

"Dr. Novak, that was amazing!" her assistant says excitedly as they leave the OR. "The way you handled that problem..."

Tamzin's face stays calm behind her mask. "Just doing my job," she replies, her voice steady despite feeling very tired.

In the scrub room, Tamzin takes off her gloves and mask. Her hands, usually so steady, shake a little as she turns on the water. The sound of running water drowns out the buzzing in her ears and the tightness in her chest.

She grips the sink tightly, eyes closed. Images flash through her mind—the patient's scared eyes before going to sleep, the tense moments when things got tricky, the huge relief when the crisis passed.

A single tear runs down her cheek. Tamzin wipes it away quickly. She feels she can't show emotions in a world where being perfect is expected.

She hears her father's voice in her head: "Novaks don't cry. Novaks don't show weakness." The mantra of her childhood, the foundation of her success.

Tamzin splashes cold water on her face, washing away any sign of her feelings. She straightens up, fixes her hair, and becomes the unshakeable Dr. Novak again.

As she leaves the scrub room, a group of young doctors walks by, laughing. For a moment, Tamzin wishes she could share her burden and not always have to be so strong.

But she pushes that thought away quickly. She has patients to see. There's no room for weakness, no time to connect with others.

Dr. Tamzin Novak walks down the hospital hallway, alone but unbreakable. Just as she's always been. Just as she feels she must always be.

The Journey Towards Vulnerability

Tamzin's story might resonate with many of us who have built walls around our emotions. Like Tamzin, I too once believed that vulnerability was a weakness to be avoided at all costs. Let me share my own journey towards embracing vulnerability.

For most of my life, vulnerability was a forbidden word. It represented all the weaknesses I refused to reveal, equating to showing emotions that left me exposed. In school, when bullied, I never allowed myself to cry. Well, almost never.

There was one incident at a birthday party when I was fourteen. Some boys began teasing me about my size. I sat on the pool steps while other girls swam or lingered nearby. The boys mocked me relentlessly, and I fought back with words, feigning indifference. But inside? I was screaming with pain. They escalated to throwing popcorn at me. To this day, I wonder why no adults stepped in to stop this cruelty. I tried to remain strong until I couldn't anymore. Tears streamed down my face as I buried my head in my hands. The boys backed away, and the nearby girls distanced themselves further. There I sat, alone and crying. That moment cemented a core belief: vulnerability wasn't a strength—it was a weakness.

This belief followed me into adulthood. In my twenties, my romantic choices were far from healthy. If I saw someone I liked with another person, I'd smile and wave as if everything was fine. When my sister passed away, I didn't shed a tear at her funeral - not because I wasn't heartbroken, but because I didn't know how to express that emotion. I had such difficulty processing the grief that I hid it in the back of my mind and told myself I needed to just continue living without my sister in my life. It took decades before I truly allowed myself to feel the full extent of the grief of losing her. During the time after her death, I became even more afraid of letting people into my life. My walls grew higher, and my fear of emotional pain became much stronger.

My thirties, spent in the corporate world, only reinforced my stoic nature. In the early 2000s, mental health wasn't a workplace topic. Emotions were meant to be checked at the reception desk, not brought into your daily routine. Any sign of vulnerability was frowned upon.

The Benefits of Embracing Vulnerability

As I entered my forties, I began to realize that my stoic approach to life was taking its toll. It wasn't until then that I finally allowed myself to cry. When I let go, I cried for all the things I hadn't before. Mainly, I grieved for my sister, realizing I'd been too young to process her death properly, building ultra-independent walls to keep the pain out. Through days of tears, I started to feel... good. You know that feeling after a good cry when you say, "Actually, I feel better for that"? As it turns out, crying triggers the parasympathetic nervous system, inducing a state of rest and relaxation. That's why many people feel better after crying. It truly does help.

As ultra-independent women, we often see vulnerable women as weak. I completely missed the benefits of being open and honest about my feelings. However, learning to embrace my vulnerability has led to amazing changes in my life—physically, emotionally, and spiritually.

The Importance of Feeling Safe

As we open up to others, we face an interesting puzzle: to be truly open, we need to feel safe, but to feel safe, we need to be open. This tricky situation is at the center of our journey to express our feelings and build real connections.

We built walls around ourselves when we were young, often because we had to. These walls protected us from getting hurt, being rejected, and feeling let down. But as time passed, these walls became like strong castles, surrounded by sharp thorns of not trusting others and being afraid. We've gotten so used to living behind these walls that we don't let anyone in anymore—not because we don't want to, but because we still don't feel safe.

The Art of Trust

For us ultra-independent women, the idea of handing over the reins to someone else is almost unthinkable. We're captaining this ship because we've seen too many icebergs to let anyone else steer. We need that control because, in our minds, trusting others means losing that control.

Learning to receive requires us to rebuild trust. Not just in others, but in ourselves and the world around us as well. It's a process of rediscovering that it's okay to be vulnerable, to ask for help when needed, and to allow others to support us. Of course, this is easier said than done.

This is especially tough if you've been burned before. Maybe you've learned the hard way that being vulnerable just leads to pain, rejection, or abandonment. Those wounds from childhood or past relationships? They make it really hard to lower our guard and open our hearts again.

But here's the beautiful truth—we have the power to rewrite these stories. We can create a new relationship with trust, one that's built on self-love, good judgment, and healthy boundaries. We can learn to trust our gut, to listen to that quiet voice inside that knows what we really need.

Trusting Your Gut: The Power of Intuition

Speaking of that little voice in your head—let's talk about intuition. For us women, our intuition is like a superpower. It's right about 99% of the time, unless it's coming from a place of past trauma or anxiety.

Your intuition isn't some mystical force. It's your brain processing a ton of information at lightning speed and coming up with the most likely outcome. It's like having a super-computer in your head, crunching data from every experience you've ever had.

Here are some tips to tune into your internal radio station:

Get quiet: Take some time each day to just be still. Meditate, journal, or just sit in silence for a few minutes.

Pay attention to your body: Notice when your stomach clenches or your shoulders tense up. Your body often knows before your mind does.

Practice mindfulness: Stay present in the moment.

Keep an intuition journal: When you get a hunch about something, write it down. Then follow up later to see if you were right.

Trust the first thought: Often, our initial reaction is the most intuitive one.

Ask yourself questions: When you're stuck, try asking yourself, "What do I know to be true about this situation?"

Act on it: The more you listen to and act on your intuition, the stronger it gets.

Vulnerability in Friendships

Now that we've explored the importance of trust and intuition, let's talk about how vulnerability plays out in our friendships. As ultra-independent women, we often worry that if we show our struggles or insecurities, or heaven forbid, ask for support, our friends might think we're weak or a burden. We've become so accustomed to being the "strong one" that the idea of letting our guard down can feel terrifying.

I remember the first time I decided to open up to my friends about my personal struggles. I was nervous, my heart racing as I shared a recent setback at work. You know what? I was blown away by their response. Not only were they incredibly supportive, but they started sharing their own vulnerabilities with me too.

It was like we'd unlocked a whole new level in our friendships. Suddenly, we weren't just hanging out and having fun—we were really connecting on a deeper level. Our conversations became richer, more meaningful. We started supporting each other through tough times and celebrating each other's victories with a new level of understanding and empathy.

By letting ourselves be vulnerable with our friends, we're actually creating space for real connection, emotional support, and personal growth. It's pretty amazing when you realize you're not alone in your struggles, and that your friends can be there for you when life gets tough.

Remember, true friendship isn't about being perfect or always having it together. It's about being real, supporting each other, and growing together. When we allow ourselves to be vulnerable, we often find that our friendships deepen, our support network strengthens, and we feel less alone in our struggles.

So, the next time you're tempted to put on your "I've got it all together" mask with your friends, try taking it off instead. You might be surprised at the genuine connections and support you'll find waiting for you.

Embracing Vulnerability in the Workplace

Just as vulnerability can deepen our friendships, it can also transform our professional lives. For many of us, the thought of being vulnerable at work seems about as appealing as showing up in our pajamas. We worry that if we reveal our true selves or admit to any difficulties or doubts, others might think we're weak, unprofessional, or incompetent. In a world where we're often told to "be confident" and project constant assurance, the idea of lowering our guard can be scary.

But genuine vulnerability can actually be a strength at work. When we let others see our human side, it builds trust and makes us more approachable. From this place of honesty, we can actually become better leaders and team members.

Let me share a personal story that shows this. When I worked in tech, a client at a big financial company called me in. They had a project that was falling behind schedule, and it was the biggest project in the building, so everyone was watching it. After looking into it, it was clear the project needed three more months and extra funding to get back on track.

The team was great—skilled professionals who were working incredibly hard to meet a deadline they knew they couldn't hit. But they were scared to admit it. I went into the boardroom with the facts, ready to deliver the news honestly and with understanding for the hardworking team.

To my surprise, the board members understood and appreciated the honesty. They preferred hearing the bad news earlier rather than later. Because of this open approach, we got more time for the team. They were able to go home for dinner with their families and rest a bit too. This experience showed me how powerful being vulnerable can be at work.

By being open and honest at work, we're showing a new kind of leadership—one that's based on understanding emotions, working together, and breaking down those old, unhealthy workplace cultures where everyone pretends to be perfect all the time. It's about creating a setting where it's okay to ask questions, admit challenges, and seek help when needed.

Here are some ways to practice vulnerability in the workplace:

- Be honest about project statuses, even when it's difficult.

- Admit when you don't know something: It's okay to say, "I'm not sure, but I'll find out."

- Share credit and acknowledge others' contributions.

- Ask for feedback and be open to constructive criticism.

- Own your mistakes: Taking responsibility when things go wrong builds trust and respect.

- Express genuine concern for your team's wellbeing.

- Ask for help when you need it: This shows trust in your team and can foster a collaborative environment.

Remember, vulnerability at work doesn't mean oversharing or being emotionally uncontrolled. It's about being authentic, honest, and human.

Overcoming the Barriers to Vulnerability

Now that we've explored the benefits of vulnerability in various aspects of our lives, you might be wondering: "Okay, so how do we actually start being more vulnerable?" It's a great question, and the answer lies in taking small, manageable steps. Here are some ideas to get you started:

- Think about what scares you about being vulnerable. What's the worst thing you think could happen if you let people see the real you?

- Start small. You don't have to bare your soul to everyone right away. Try sharing something small but real with someone you trust. Maybe a minor worry or a small fear.

- Remember that little kid inside you who learned it wasn't okay to have feelings or need help? It might be time to have a chat with her and let her know it's safe now.

- Be kind to yourself as you start this journey. Celebrate every small step you take towards being more open and vulnerable. It's not easy, but you're doing great.

Stella's Story: Finding Safety in Unexpected Places

To illustrate how these principles can work in practice, let me share the story of my client, Stella, and her journey towards feeling secure and embracing vulnerability.

When Stella first walked into my office, I could almost see the invisible armor she wore. Like many ultra-independent women I've worked with, she carried herself with a kind of rigid strength. As we dug into her past, it became clear why she'd built such sturdy walls around herself.

Stella shook her head as she recounted her childhood experiences. "I was basically the family's adult from age nine," she said. "My mom would drop me off at the laundromat to do everyone's laundry. Can you imagine? A nine-year-old kid, responsible for keeping the whole family in clean clothes!"

I knew we had to start small, so I introduced Stella to the idea of creating a 'Safe Container'—a personal space where she could begin to feel secure and gradually let others in on her own terms. We broke it down into three parts:

Physical Safety:

"Where do you feel most comfortable?" I asked her. Stella's answer surprised us both.

"You know what's weird?" she said with a little laugh. "I actually love doing laundry now. It's the one place where I feel totally in control."

So, we decided to run with it. Stella turned her laundry room into a mini-sanctuary, complete with a comfy chair, a soft rug, and some potted plants. Her own little oasis of calm.

Emotional Safety:

This was trickier. I asked Stella to think about the last time she felt truly accepted.

"When was the last time you were with someone and thought, 'I can just be me right now'?" I prompted.

After some thought, Stella mentioned her friend Sarah and her cousin Mike. We made a plan for her to spend more quality time with them, starting with weekly coffee dates with Sarah.

Psychological Safety:

Here, we focused on boundaries. I taught Stella what I like to call the 'Pause Button Technique'.

"Next time you feel overwhelmed," I explained, "imagine hitting a giant pause button on life. Take a deep breath, count to five. Then ask yourself: What am I feeling? Why? How do I want to handle this?"

We practiced this in our sessions, role-playing scenarios where Stella felt pressured or uncomfortable. It was like watching her find her footing, step by step.

To help Stella build inner safety, we also tried the 5-4-3-2-1 grounding technique. It became a bit of a game in our sessions:

"Okay, Stella," I'd say, "what are 5 things you can see right now?"

She'd look around my office. "Your messy bookshelf, that sad-looking plant in the corner, the weird abstract painting, the clock that's always five minutes fast, and my own sweaty hands."

We'd go through the rest of the senses, and by the end, Stella would be noticeably calmer. "It's like I was floating before," she once said, "and now I'm back in my body."

As we kept working together, we tried out more exercises:

The Emotion Diary:

Stella started keeping track of her feelings each day. "Don't judge them," I said. "Just name them. Like, 'Today I felt annoyed at my boss, happy about my lunch, and worried about my to-do list.'"

Body Boundary Meditation:

We practiced imagining a warm, protective light around her body. Stella found this helpful before family gatherings, which she used to dread.

Vulnerability 'Baby Steps':

I encouraged Stella to share small, real things with people she trusted. She started by telling Sarah about a work worry. "Sarah was so supportive," Stella told me later, sounding surprised and pleased.

Safety Affirmations:

Stella's favorite became, "I carry my safety within me, like a warm, freshly laundered blanket." It was cheesy, but it worked for her.

The Empathy Challenge:

For a week, Stella tried to see things from others' perspectives. "When someone cuts you off in traffic," I suggested, "instead of getting mad, try thinking, 'Maybe they're rushing to the hospital.'"

Slowly but surely, Stella's sense of safety started to grow beyond her laundry room. She began to feel more comfortable in different situations and started opening up in her relationships.

"You won't believe this," Stella said in one of our later sessions, "but I actually told Sarah about my childhood the other day. I was scared, but it felt... good. Like I was finally letting someone see the real me."

It wasn't an overnight change, but each small step was a victory in Stella's journey. She was rewriting her story—from a kid forced to grow up too fast to a woman creating her own sense of safety and connection. And let me tell you, watching that transformation was pretty amazing.

Final Thoughts

As we've explored in this chapter, embracing vulnerability is a journey that involves rebuilding trust, tuning into our intuition, and creating safe spaces for ourselves and others. It's about rewriting our stories and challenging the belief that vulnerability equals weakness. Instead, we've seen how it can be a source of strength, deepening our relationships, improving our physical and mental health, and fostering personal growth.

Remember, this journey is unique for each of us. What worked for Stella or for me might look different for you. The key is to start small, be patient with yourself, and celebrate each step forward. As you continue on this path, you may find, like I did, that vulnerability isn't just about showing your emotions or asking for help—it's about living authentically, connecting deeply, and embracing the full spectrum of human experience.

So, my fellow ultra-independent women, I invite you to take that first step. Open up a little. Trust a little more. And watch as your world expands in ways you never imagined possible.

Exercises and Reflection Questions:

To help you on your journey towards embracing vulnerability, here are some exercises and reflection questions you can try:

Exercise 1: Safe Space Visualization:

Close your eyes and imagine a place where you feel completely safe and at peace. Engage all your senses. What do you see, hear, smell, feel, and taste? Practice visiting this place in your mind whenever you need to feel calm and secure.

Exercise 2: The Emotion Diary:

For one week, keep a daily log of your emotions. Name at least three different emotions each day. This exercise helps build emotional awareness, a key component of both safety and vulnerability.

Exercise 3: Body Boundary Meditation:

Sit comfortably and imagine a warm, protective light surrounding your body. As you breathe in, feel this light strengthening your personal boundaries. As you breathe out, feel any tension or fear leaving your body.

Exercise 4: Vulnerability "Baby Steps":

Start with sharing something small but real with a person you trust. It could be a minor worry or a small personal victory. Notice how it feels to open up, even in this small way.

Exercise 5: The Pause Button Technique:

When you're in a heated situation, imagine hitting a giant pause button. Take a deep breath and ask yourself: "What am I feeling right now? Why am I feeling this way? How do I want to respond?" This technique helps create a sense of safety in challenging moments and allows space for vulnerability.

Exercise 6: Safety Affirmations Mirror Work:

Stand in front of a mirror and speak safety affirmations out loud, such as "I am safe in my own body" or "I trust my ability to protect myself." As you grow more comfortable with these, try adding vulnerability-focused affirmations like "It's okay to let others see the real me."

Exercise 7: The Empathy Challenge:

For one week, make it your mission to see things from other people's perspectives. This exercise builds both safety (by helping you understand others better) and vulnerability (by encouraging you to connect more deeply with others' experiences).

Exercise 8: Trust Temperature Check Worksheet:

Create a worksheet with key areas of your life: self-trust, trust in relationships, trust at work, and trust in the universe. Score each area from 1-10 based on how much you trust in that area. Reflect on your scores and identify areas where you might want to focus on building more trust.

Exercise 9: "I Trusted Someone and Lived to Tell the Tale" Story Time:

Reflect on a time when you took a chance and trusted someone, even though it felt scary. Write down what happened, how you felt, and what you learned from the experience.

Exercise 10: Self-Trust Pep Talk Meditation:

Find a quiet spot and visualize yourself making decisions with confidence, treating yourself with kindness, and setting healthy boundaries. Focus on the feelings of self-assurance and self-respect this brings.

Reflection Questions:

1. What beliefs or stories do you hold about receiving support or care from others? Where do these beliefs come from, and how have they impacted your relationships and well-being?

2. Recall a time when you allowed yourself to receive support or care from someone else, even if it felt uncomfortable. What did you learn from that experience? How did it impact your relationship with that person?

3. Think about a relationship where you would like to build greater trust. What small steps could you take to practice vulnerability and open communication with that person?

4. Reflect on your own emotional intelligence. What are your strengths in this area, and where do you have room for growth? What practices or tools could support you in cultivating greater self-awareness and empathy?

5. What's one small step you could take this week to practice vulnerability, even if it scares you a bit?

6. How might getting curious about—rather than judging—your emotional experiences foster greater self-awareness?

7. In what areas of your life could embracing vulnerability and cultivating safety

serve you and those around you?

8. Call to mind a situation where you were hard on yourself recently for a mistake or imperfection. How might you extend yourself the compassion you would offer a dear friend in the same circumstances?

9. Which safety affirmations resonated most deeply with you? How might reciting them remind you of your fundamental wholeness and worthiness?

Remember, learning to receive, trust, and cultivate emotional intelligence is a brave and beautiful act of self-love. It's a way of honoring your own worthiness and inviting more love, abundance, and connection into your life. And as you open yourself up to receive more fully, you also create space for others to do the same—rippling out healing and wholeness in ever-widening circles.

So be gentle with yourself on this journey. Take it one step at a time, and trust that each act of receiving is planting a seed of love and resilience within you. You are worthy of all the support, care, and nourishment this life has to offer. Believe in your own capacity to receive it gracefully—and watch in wonder as your world begins to blossom in response.

Now that we have begun to embrace vulnerability and trust, let's continue on this journey by learning to accept help from others in the next chapter.

Chapter Twelve

Accepting Help

The next time someone offers you a gift, whether it's a potted plant or a heartfelt compliment, take a deep breath and allow yourself to receive it fully.

Sarah's Story: The Overwhelmed Overachiever

Sarah collapses onto her sofa, exhausted after another frantic day at the office. Her mind races, filled with endless to-do lists and deadlines that seem insurmountable. Her iPhone buzzes constantly with missed calls and messages from her best friend, sister, and colleagues, all vying for her attention. But Sarah can't bring herself to answer. The thought of them discovering she's struggling is unbearable.

She's always been the one with her act together. At work, she's the go-to person for the toughest projects and most demanding deadlines. In her personal life, she's the rock, the fixer, the one everyone relies on. Yet, sitting alone in her apartment, Sarah feels crushed under the weight of her own expectations.

What would they think if they knew the truth? That behind her polished exterior and can-do attitude, she's just as lost and overwhelmed as anyone else? Her phone chirps again—it's her sister, checking in. For a fleeting moment, Sarah's finger hovers over the reply button, aching to admit she's struggling and needs help.

But the words stick in her throat. Instead, she taps out a quick lie, telling her sister everything's fine, just buried under work. As she hits send, guilt washes over her. She knows she's lying, not just to her sister, but to herself. Asking for help feels like admitting weakness, and Sarah learned long ago that weakness isn't an option if she wants to survive in this dog-eat-dog world.

So Sarah soldiers on, shoulders back, chin up. Alone, always alone, no matter how heavy the load gets.

The Roots of Resistance: Why We're So Stubborn

We've been let down more times than we can count. Parents who were supposed to be our rock turned out to be unreliable. Best friends spilled our secrets faster than we could blink. Colleagues threw us under the bus to save their own skin. Lovers who promised forever barely made it past Tuesday.

With each disappointment and betrayal, we built our walls higher and made our circle tighter. We became the architects of our own fortresses, determined to control every brick, every entrance, every exit.

For us, the world is a harsh and unforgiving place. We've learned the hard way that the only person we can truly count on is the one staring back at us in the mirror. That's why we've created these safety bubbles—small, manageable, and most importantly, ours. Asking for help feels like inviting chaos into our carefully ordered lives. It's dangerous, unpredictable, and frankly, terrifying.

In the past, I never asked for help. Ever. I just didn't trust others enough because people had let me down repeatedly. I believed that asking for help would make me look less like the superhero I strived to be, and I was convinced that I should be able to do everything myself—that I could handle any situation better than anyone else.

During the planning of a weekend trip with my friends, we encountered a problem. They all wanted to leave on Friday morning, but I had to pick up my son from school.

One of them, a friend of a friend, suggested, "Why not ask someone else to pick him up?"

I was caught off guard. "Who?" I asked.

She looked at me with surprise. "There must be someone you can ask," she insisted.

"I don't have anyone," I replied truthfully.

The idea of having a backup plan or support system is foreign to me—and probably to you as well, right?

But sometimes life forces our hand. Let me tell you another story:

While in England scouting schools for my son before our move from South Africa, my 87-year-old mother, who was caring for my 13-year-old son, became extremely ill and had to spend the night in the hospital.

I was stuck. I'm from a small family, so there are no relatives nearby, and there was no magic means of piloting an aircraft back to Cape Town. I found myself with no option but to ask for help from a friend.

With hesitation and fear, I reached out to her. She responded with such kindness, picking up my son and even staying with him for a whole week. Her generosity went beyond my expectations. It took being miles away for me to finally ask for help, but it taught me a valuable lesson: There are compassionate people out there, even if they may be rare to come by.

The Gift of Receiving: Learning to Accept Without Guilt

For us ultra-independents, receiving can feel downright uncomfortable. I noticed this weird pattern in myself. Someone would treat me to dinner or buy me a little something, and instead of enjoying it, my brain would immediately start racing. "How can I pay them back? What do I owe them now?" Sound familiar? It's like we can't just sit back and enjoy the moment without feeling guilty.

One incident, in particular, made me realize this more clearly. I was walking back from the store with a fake cactus I'd bought for my son. A young man commented on it, and we got chatting. He offered to give me a real cactus from his collection.

Instead of just appreciating his kindness, I went home and picked out a crystal to give him in return. When he arrived with the potted cactus, I immediately handed him the crystal. He seemed to like it, but I realized I'd taken away from his gesture by not simply receiving.

This is a struggle many of us face. We're so used to being the givers that accepting without immediately reciprocating feels almost selfish. But when we do this, we're actually diminishing the giver's joy.

So here's my challenge to you: next time someone offers you something, whether it's a gift or a compliment, just accept it. Look them in the eye, smile, and say thank you. That's it. No mental calculations about how to pay them back.

It might feel weird at first, but with practice, it gets easier. You might find your relationships deepening and your life enriched in unexpected ways.

Remember, graciously receiving isn't selfish - it's allowing someone else to experience the joy of giving. And that, my friend, is a beautiful thing.

And then, when the time is right, find a way to pay it forward. Not because you owe them anything, but because you understand the beauty and power of generosity. By opening yourself up to receive, you're creating more space for love, abundance, and connection to flow in all directions.

Trust me, this is a practice that gets easier with time. As you start to embrace receiving with more ease and grace, you'll find that your relationships deepen, your heart expands, and your life becomes infinitely richer in all the ways that truly matter.

The Cultural Context

As women, we might have been taught to always put others first, caring for everyone else before ourselves. People of color might feel they need to be extra strong to deal with unfair treatment. And LGBTQ+ folks might have learned to protect themselves in a world that's not always welcoming, relying only on themselves and close friends for support.

These old habits of doing everything ourselves and always putting others first run deep. They shape how we think and act, often without us realizing it. This can show up as:

- Not wanting to ask for help, even when things are tough.

- Taking on too much, more than we can handle.

- Being afraid of looking needy or dependent, or losing our independence.

But getting help isn't a weakness. It actually takes a lot of strength to be open and let others support us. It shows we understand that we're all connected, and that we get better together.

Learning to accept help is also a powerful way to push back against a society that tells us we always need to be doing, achieving, and standing on our own to be worthy. By letting ourselves receive help, we challenge these limiting ideas and open up to a more balanced and satisfying way of living.

Learning to Receive: Anastasia's Journey

Meet Anastasia, a sales executive and single mom who came to me struggling with burnout and feelings of isolation. On the surface, she had it all together - a thriving career, a beautiful home, and an adorable 6-year-old son. But beneath that polished exterior, Anastasia was drowning.

"I just can't bring myself to ask for help," she confessed during our first session. "Every time I think about reaching out, I hear my mom's voice in my head telling me I'm being a burden."

As we dug deeper, Anastasia revealed that growing up, her mother would often sigh dramatically and say things like, "I guess I'll do it myself since no one else will help around here." This left Anastasia with a deep-seated belief that asking for help was an inconvenience to others.

"I don't want to be like my mom, always complaining," Anastasia explained. "So I just do everything myself. But I'm exhausted, and I feel so alone."

We started small, with a simple exercise I call the "Help Inventory." I asked Anastasia to keep a log for a week, noting every time she needed help but didn't ask for it. Next to each instance, she wrote down what she imagined would happen if she did ask for help, and then what might realistically happen.

When we reviewed her log, a pattern emerged. Anastasia consistently imagined worst-case scenarios - people getting angry, feeling burdened, or thinking less of her. But when we explored more realistic outcomes, she began to see that most people in her life would likely be happy to help.

Our next step was to challenge these beliefs with real-world experiments. I encouraged Anastasia to start with low-stakes requests. She began by asking a colleague to proofread an important email, something she'd always done herself in the past.

"It was terrifying," Anastasia admitted in our next session. "But you know what? Sarah was happy to help. She even thanked me for trusting her with the task."

Encouraged by this success, we gradually increased the stakes. Anastasia asked her neighbor to watch her son for an hour so she could go to a doctor's appointment. She reached out to a friend for help moving some furniture. Each time, she was met with enthusiasm rather than the reluctance she had feared.

As Anastasia practiced receiving help, she also worked on building her emotional intelligence. We used mindfulness techniques to help her tune into her body's signals of stress and overwhelm. She learned to recognize when she was reaching her limits and to view asking for help as an act of self-care rather than a sign of weakness.

One of our breakthrough moments came when Anastasia's son fell ill, and she had a crucial presentation at work. In the past, she would have tried to do it all - care for her son, prepare for the presentation, and run herself ragged in the process.

This time, she took a deep breath and called her best friend. "I need help," she said, her voice shaking. "Can you come over and stay with Tommy while I finish my work?"

Her friend's response brought tears to Anastasia's eyes: "Of course! I've been waiting for you to ask. I'm so glad you reached out."

That night, as her son slept peacefully and her presentation was prepared, Anastasia realized something. "People want to help," she told me in our next session. "When I ask for help, I'm not just receiving support - I'm giving others the gift of being able to contribute."

Over time, Anastasia built a network of support - friends, neighbors, and colleagues who she could rely on, and who knew they could rely on her too. She learned that interdependence wasn't a weakness, but a strength that allowed her to show up more fully in all areas of her life.

"I used to think being strong meant doing everything alone," Anastasia reflected in one of our later sessions. "Now I know that true strength lies in being vulnerable enough to ask for and receive help when I need it."

Anastasia's journey shows us that learning to receive is a process. It takes time, patience, and practice. But with each small step, we open ourselves up to a world of support, connection, and shared strength. Remember, asking for help isn't a burden - it's an invitation for others to be part of your journey, and a powerful affirmation of our shared humanity.

Embracing Interdependence

As we learn to receive and build trust, we also begin to recognize the power of interdependence—the idea that we are all part of a vast web of connection and support, and that our strength lies not in doing everything alone, but in reaching out and asking for help when we need it.

Interdependence means recognizing that we need each other to thrive and that there is strength in collaboration and mutual support. It means building a network of supportive friends, family members, and community allies who can be there for us in times of need. It means seeking out mentors and role models who can offer guidance and wisdom on our journeys. And it means being willing to offer our own support and care to others, in whatever ways we can.

This doesn't mean giving up our autonomy or independence; rather, it means embracing a more balanced and interconnected way of being. It means recognizing that we are all in this together and that our individual and collective well-being is deeply intertwined.

Exercises and Reflection Questions:

Exercise 1: Practice small acts of receiving:

This week, look for opportunities to receive support or care in small ways. Notice any resistance or discomfort that comes up, and get curious about it. Allow yourself to fully receive the support and notice how it feels in your body and heart.

Exercise 2: Help Inventory:

For one week, keep a log of every time you need help but don't ask for it.

Use the following format:

- Situation: Briefly describe what you needed help with.

- Why I didn't ask: Note your reasons for not asking for help.

- Imagined outcome: What did you think would happen if you asked?

- Realistic outcome: What might realistically happen if you asked?

At the end of the week, review your log.

- Look for patterns in your thinking and behavior.

- Are there certain types of help you're more reluctant to ask for?

- Are your imagined outcomes overly negative compared to the realistic ones?

Use these insights to challenge your beliefs and gradually start asking for help in low-stakes situations.

Exercise 3: Write a letter to your younger self:

Imagine you could go back in time and offer love, support, and encouragement to your younger self.

- What would you say?

- How would you reassure and nurture them?

Writing this letter can be a powerful way to practice self-compassion and deepen your connection to your own inner wisdom.

Exercise 4: Reach out for support:

Identify a challenge or area in your life where you could use some support. Reach out to someone you trust and ask for their help or guidance. Notice how it feels to ask for and receive their support, and reflect on what you learn from the experience.

Exercise 5: Gratitude for Support Received:

At the end of each day, write down three instances where you received help or support, no matter how small. This could be anything from someone holding a door open for you to a friend offering advice. Reflect on how it felt to receive this support and express gratitude for it.

Reflection:

1. What beliefs do you hold about receiving support or care from others? Where do these beliefs come from?

2. Recall a time when you received support, even if it felt uncomfortable. What did you learn from that experience?

3. Think about a relationship in your life where you want to build greater trust. What small steps could you take to practice vulnerability and open communication in that relationship?

4. Reflect on your own emotional intelligence. What are your strengths and areas for growth?

As we've learned to open ourselves to the help of others, we've laid the groundwork for perhaps the most important relationship of all—the one with ourselves. In the next chapter, we'll explore the transformative power of self-love and how it can reshape our ultra-independent tendencies, helping us to embrace our whole, authentic selves with compassion and grace.

Chapter Thirteen

The Power of Self Love

Self-love is not a solitary pursuit, but a wellspring from which we draw the courage to open ourselves to the love and support of others.

Mia's Story: The Struggle Within

The harsh fluorescent light flickers as Mia stares at her reflection in the office bathroom mirror. Dark circles rim her eyes, a testament to another sleepless night spent poring over work reports. She pinches the skin around her waist, frowning at the imagined imperfections.

Earlier that day, Mia had thrown herself into a new client project with frantic energy. Her employees marveled at her ability, but they didn't see the desperation behind her drive. Each successful presentation, each word of praise from her team, was a temporary balm for the ache of unworthiness that gnawed at her core.

Her phone buzzes. It's her mother. Again. Mia's stomach tightens as she ignores the notification, not wanting to read the text. She can picture the scene at her mother's house all too well - empty wine bottles, unwashed dishes, and a mother too inebriated to stand.

As she grabs her keys to head out for her date, another text pings through. This time, it's her father. "Can't make it this weekend. Something came up at work." Mia's heart sinks. It's been months since his last visit, yet the sting of disappointment feels fresh every time.

Now, Mia finds herself at a bar, nursing a drink as she waits for her date. He's late. Again. But Mia will wait, just as she always does. Because when he does show up, when he flashes that charming smile and tells her she looks beautiful, for a moment she'll feel seen. Wanted. Even if she knows, deep down, that he'll never truly value her.

As the night wears on and her date's attention wanders to other women in the bar, Mia makes a mental list of all the ways she needs to improve. Work harder. Look better. Be more interesting. The list is endless, a perpetual cycle of self-improvement that never quite leads to self-acceptance.

Back home, Mia collapses onto her bed, exhaustion seeping into her bones. Her gaze falls on the self-help book gathering dust on her nightstand. "5 Minutes to Self-Love," the title proclaims. Mia almost laughs. Self-love? When would she have time for that? Between worrying about her mother, chasing her father's approval, running her company, and trying to make her relationships last, there's no space left for herself.

As she drifts off to sleep, a small voice in the back of her mind whispers a truth she's not ready to hear: in all her efforts to be loved, to be enough for everyone else, she's completely neglected the most important relationship of all - the one with herself.

Just like Mia, we've spent so long putting everyone else first, priding ourselves on our ability to handle everything solo, that the idea of prioritizing our own needs can seem selfish or even weak. But it's important to understand that self-love isn't just important for us—it's absolutely essential.

Reconnecting to our authentic selves

For many of us ultra-independent women, our lives revolve around seeking validation from external sources—our careers, relationships, and achievements. We've become experts at meeting others' expectations, often at the expense of our own well-being. This pattern, however, can be broken by learning to value ourselves intrinsically, not just for what we can do or achieve.

We often equate strength with the ability to do everything alone. But true strength lies in knowing when to ask for help, when to rest, and when to prioritize our own needs. By redefining strength on our own terms, we allow ourselves to be both fierce and vulnerable, independent and connected.

Many of us developed our ultra-independent tendencies as a response to past hurts or traumas. Acknowledging and healing these wounds, rather than pushing them aside in our relentless drive forward, is crucial for our personal growth.

When we prioritize our own worth, we naturally set healthier boundaries in our relationships. We become less likely to accept treatment that doesn't align with our value, and more likely to attract and maintain fulfilling connections with others who respect us.

This shift in self-perception isn't just about feeling good—it has tangible benefits for our mental, emotional, and even physical health. When we practice self-care and self-compassion, we're better equipped to handle stress, more resilient in the face of challenges, and more likely to make choices that support our overall well-being.

As leaders in our families, workplaces, and communities, embracing our own worth models essential behavior for others, particularly the next generation of women and girls. It teaches us to embrace our imperfections rather than constantly striving for an unattainable ideal. This doesn't mean we stop growing or improving, but rather that we approach our personal development from a place of acceptance and compassion instead of harsh self-criticism.

In our drive to meet others' needs and expectations, many of us have lost touch with our own desires, passions, and dreams. By reconnecting with our authentic selves, we create space to rediscover what truly brings us joy and fulfillment.

For us ultra-independent women, cultivating a deep sense of self-worth isn't just a nice-to-have—it's a radical act of self-preservation and empowerment. It's about reclaiming our right to prioritize ourselves, to value our own well-being as much as we value others'. As we'll explore in the rest of this chapter, learning to love ourselves deeply and unconditionally is perhaps the most important journey we can undertake.

Reconnecting with Our Authentic Selves

In our drive to meet others' needs and expectations, many of us have lost touch with our own desires, passions, and dreams. By reconnecting with our authentic selves, we create space to rediscover what truly brings us joy and fulfillment.

Cultivating a deep sense of self-worth isn't just a nice-to-have—it's a radical act of self-preservation and empowerment. It's about reclaiming our right to prioritize ourselves, to value our own well-being as much as we value others'.

The Journey to Self-Love: One Step at a Time

Let me introduce you to my client Sabrina. She's a 42-year-old business owner who came to me feeling lost after her divorce. Sabrina had spent her life putting everyone else first. She'd never really learned how to love and care for herself. When we started working together, she was feeling adrift, unsure of who she even was anymore.

I explained to Sabrina that self-love isn't a destination we arrive at one day. It's a lifelong commitment, with ups and downs. It takes patience, practice, and a willingness to face parts of ourselves we've been avoiding.

Honesty

First, I encouraged Sabrina to get honest with herself. We worked on developing self-awareness that, I warned her, might be uncomfortable at times. We needed to look at her thoughts, feelings, and behaviors, and how they were impacting her sense of self-worth. As an exercise, I had her refrain from gossiping about herself for three days. Every time she caught herself saying something negative internally, I asked her to pause and simply acknowledge the thought without trying to change it. Sabrina was surprised by how often she criticized herself in her own head.

Beliefs and Patterns

We then looked at uncovering beliefs and patterns that were no longer serving her, like equating her worth with how productive she was. But as we worked through this, Sabrina started to see how empowering self-awareness could be. She began making conscious choices about how she wanted to show up in the world, identifying areas for healing and growth, and supporting herself with compassion.

Self-Acceptance: Embracing Your Perfectly Imperfect Self

Now, let's talk about self-acceptance. It's a crucial piece of the self-love puzzle, especially for us ultra-independent women. It means embracing all parts of ourselves, quirks and flaws included. It's about recognizing our inherent worth as human beings.

For Sabrina, this was challenging. Like many of us, she'd spent years trying to be flawless. Any perceived weakness was seen as a failure, something to be fixed or hidden away.

We worked on reframing her perspective. Instead of seeing imperfections as liabilities, we started viewing them as unique aspects of her humanity. For instance, Sabrina's tendency to overthink, which she had always seen as a flaw, we reframed as thoughtfulness and attention to detail.

I helped her realize that embracing our full humanity is actually a strength. When we show up authentically, we create space for genuine connection and growth. This was a revelation for Sabrina, who had always equated vulnerability with weakness.

We practiced self-acceptance exercises, like naming things she loved about herself - both physical attributes and personality traits. At first, Sabrina struggled with this. But as we kept at it, she found it easier to recognize and appreciate her unique qualities.

Remember, self-acceptance doesn't mean we're giving up on growth. It's about loving yourself enough to grow from a place of self-compassion rather than self-criticism. It's about acknowledging that you're worthy of love and respect, exactly as you are, while still being open to change.

Harnessing the Power of Affirmations and the RAS

To help Sabrina cultivate self-love, we turned to affirmations. By consistently affirming her worth, Sabrina could rewire those self-sabotaging thought patterns and nurture a more loving inner dialogue.

We created personalized affirmations for Sabrina, like "I am worthy of love and respect, regardless of my achievements" and "My needs and desires matter." I taught her about the Reticular Activating System (RAS) (which we discussed in the chapter about Family dynamics) and how repeating these statements could help reprogram her subconscious mind to focus on self-love and acceptance.

Sabrina practiced these affirmations daily. At first, she felt awkward and didn't believe the words. But over time, she noticed a shift. She began to catch herself in moments of negative self-talk and replace those thoughts with her affirmations.

As Sabrina progressed, she began to notice changes in how she treated herself and interacted with others. She started setting boundaries at work, took up a hobby she had always wanted to try, and even began dating again - this time with a clearer sense of her own worth and what she deserved in a relationship.

Overcoming the Guilt of Self-Love

We then moved onto removing the guilt Sabrina had associated with self love and self care.

We worked on reframing self-love as a necessity rather than a luxury. I asked Sabrina to imagine she was a car. "If you never put gas in the tank, change the oil, or perform regular maintenance, what would happen?" She quickly realized that without proper care, she'd break down.

We practiced self-love activities, starting small. Sabrina began by taking five minutes each day to do something solely for herself - reading a book, taking a short walk, or simply sitting in silence. As she got more comfortable, we increased the time and variety of self-love practices.

The Power of Self-Love in Releasing Ultra-Independence

As Sabrina progressed in her self-love journey, she began to notice a shift in her ultra-independent behaviors. She found that loving herself made it easier to ask for help when she needed it. She realized that true strength wasn't about doing everything alone, but about knowing when to lean on others.

We worked on identifying areas where her ultra-independence was serving her and areas where it was holding her back. Sabrina learned that she could maintain her autonomy and strength while also allowing herself to be vulnerable and connected with others.

For example, Sabrina had always prided herself on handling her business entirely on her own. But as she cultivated self-love, she realized that delegating tasks wasn't a sign of weakness, but a smart business decision that allowed her to focus on her strengths. She hired an assistant and found that not only did her stress levels decrease, but her business actually grew as a result.

Putting It All Together

Cultivating self-love as an ultra-independent woman involves developing self-awareness, practicing self-acceptance, using affirmations, reprogramming limiting beliefs, prioritizing self-care, setting healthy boundaries, and surrounding yourself with supportive people and resources.

It's a process of unlearning old patterns, healing past wounds, and embracing your inherent worthiness. It requires courage, compassion, and a willingness to show up for yourself, even when it feels uncomfortable.

But know this: every small step you take towards loving yourself more deeply is powerful. As you reclaim your own worth, you inspire other women to do the same. You become a force for positive change in this world.

So keep showing up for yourself, keep affirming your worth, keep expanding your capacity for joy and connection. Trust that you are exactly where you need to be on this journey, and that your desire for wholeness is a valid and important calling.

Exercise and Reflection Questions:

Exercise 1: Unpacking Your Self-Love Baggage:

- Reflect on your childhood. What messages did you receive about self-care and prioritizing your own needs? Write down 2-3 specific memories or messages that stand out.

- Think about your current life. Where do you see these early messages influencing your behavior now? How do they impact your ability to practice self-love?

- Imagine your best friend was in your shoes. What advice would you give them about self-love and self-care? How does it feel to extend that same compassion to yourself?

- Write a letter to your younger self, offering the love and support you needed back then. What would you say to reassure and encourage that younger version of you?

Exercise 2: Creating Your Self-Love Ritual

Here's a simple framework to get you started:

Find a quiet moment: It could be first thing in the morning, during your lunch break, or before bed. The key is consistency.

Ground yourself: Take a few deep breaths, feel your feet on the floor, and bring your awareness to the present moment.

Mirror work: Look at yourself in the mirror and say one of your affirmations out loud. Really look into your own eyes as you say it.

Gratitude: List three things you're grateful for about yourself today. They can be big or small.

Self-compassion: Place a hand on your heart and offer yourself some words of kindness, as you would to a dear friend.

Set an intention: Choose one way you'll show yourself love today, no matter how small.

Reflections:

1. What are three non-negotiable ways you can prioritize self-care this week? How can you lovingly hold yourself accountable?

2. What beliefs do you carry about self-love being selfish or frivolous? Where did you learn these, and how are they holding you back?

3. Where do you need to set more loving boundaries in your life and relationships? What scares you about drawing these lines?

4. What would your life look like if you were radically committed to your own unconditional thriving? What would need to change?

5. How can you bring more playfulness and joy into your daily routine? What replenishes your spirit?

Self-Worth Affirmations with RAS:

Complete these statements and select 4 that resonate with you. Repeat your chosen statements to yourself each evening for the next two weeks.

I am loved because

I am wanted because

I am supported because

I am smart because

I am strong because

I belong in this body and in this space because

I make others happy because

I accept myself because

I am secure because

I am worthy of love because

I attract abundance into my life because

I am respected because

I am beautiful because

I am full of gratitude because

I attract opportunities because

I am a positive light because

I am kind because

I love myself because

I am safe because

I am grounded because

I am learning new things about myself everyday because

I walk with love in my heart because

I am enough because

Remember, your journey to self-love is a return to your own innate wholeness. Trust the process, be gentle with yourself, and know that you are supported every step of the way. You've got this, my fierce, independent friend. Here's to falling in love with the amazing woman you are!

With a foundation of self-love in place, we're ready to explore the delicate dance of energies within us. In the next chapter, we'll dive into the balance of masculine and feminine, learning how to harmonize these forces for a more integrated sense of self.

Chapter Fourteen

Masculine and Feminine – The Balancing Act

We are not meant to choose between our inner warrior and our inner nurturer – our power lies in embracing both.

Linda's Story: The Price of Fitting In

The clinking of glasses and roar of laughter fill the dimly lit restaurant as Linda takes her seat at the executive team dinner. She smooths her skirt and adjusts her blazer, her polished appearance a stark contrast to the sea of suits surrounding her.

As the only woman at the table, Linda is accustomed to being an outsider. The conversation flows, the jokes becoming more raucous and crude as the evening wears on.

Linda joins in, her laughter ringing out above the others. She matches their banter, throwing out a few bold quips of her own. The men nod approvingly, their eyes glinting with something like respect.

But as Linda reaches for her wine glass, she catches a glimpse of her reflection in the polished silver. The woman staring back at her is almost unrecognizable, her features hard and angular, her smile more of a smirk.

Is this what it takes to succeed in this world? Linda wonders, a sinking feeling in her gut. To become one of the boys, to suppress her feminine energy and embrace the aggressive, unyielding masculine?

She thinks back to her early days in the company, the long hours spent poring over marketing strategies and campaign ideas. She remembers how her male colleagues would talk over her in meetings, dismissing her suggestions with condescending chuckles.

Linda learned quickly that to be heard, she needed to speak their language. She started dressing sharper, her heels higher, her handshake firmer. She stopped prefacing her opinions with "I think" or "Maybe we could," instead stating them as unassailable facts.

And it worked. Linda rose through the ranks, earning a reputation as a tough, no-nonsense leader. She was invited to boys' nights out, her presence at the poker table or golf course a testament to her status as "one of them."

But now, as Linda sits at this table, surrounded by the trappings of her success, she feels a hollow ache in her chest. She thinks of her husband, the way his eyes sometimes flicker with hurt when she shoots down his ideas or dismisses his concerns. She thinks of the friendships she's let fade away, the hobbies and passions she's abandoned in pursuit of her career.

Is this the price of fitting in? Linda wonders, her grip tightening on her glass. Is this the cost of being taken seriously in a man's world?

The conversation around her grows louder, more raucous. The men are telling a particularly lewd joke, their laughter booming across the restaurant. Linda joins in, but her laughter feels forced, her smile brittle.

She excuses herself to the restroom, her steps unsteady in her high heels. As she stands in front of the mirror, she takes a deep breath, trying to calm her racing heart.

The woman staring back at her looks tired, her eyes shadowed and skin pale under the harsh fluorescent lights. Linda hardly recognizes herself, this hard, unyielding version of the woman she once was.

She thinks of the little girl she used to be, the one who dreamed of changing the world with her creativity and compassion. She thinks of the woman she could be, if only she had the courage to embrace her feminine energy, to lead with empathy and intuition.

But the thought of letting go, of showing vulnerability in front of her colleagues, fills Linda with terror. She's worked too hard to get where she is, fought too long to be taken seriously. She can't risk losing it all now.

With a deep breath, Linda straightens her shoulders and walks out of the restroom, her mask of calm confidence firmly back in place. She returns to the table, to the laughter and crude jokes, to the world she's fought so hard to be a part of.

But deep inside, a small voice whispers that this isn't the life she wants, that there must be another way.

Understanding Masculine and Feminine Energies

As ultra-independents, we often find ourselves living primarily in our masculine energy. This isn't surprising - it's the energy of doing, achieving, and overcoming challenges. It's what has helped us survive and thrive in a demanding world. But what if embracing our feminine side could help us grow even more?

Everyone has both masculine and feminine traits, regardless of their gender or appearance. This isn't about conforming to specific definitions of man or woman; instead, it's about using different energies to navigate life effectively.

- Masculine energy is about action and progress. It helps us set goals, make decisions, and overcome challenges.

- Feminine energy is about being present and self-aware. It helps us feel, adapt, and build connections.

Both energies are important. The key is finding a balance and using each energy when needed, without hiding parts of ourselves.

Picture an ancient village. Men build homes, find food, and protect the community. Women care for children, solve conflicts, and offer emotional support. Both roles were vital for survival. Today, we still need both energies to thrive. But as ultra-independents, we might rely too heavily on masculine energy to get by. We might even push away our feminine side, thinking it's not as useful or important.

It's crucial to recognize that while both masculine and feminine energies are valuable, they can have downsides too, especially when we're stressed or afraid:

- Masculine energy might turn into being bossy, aggressive, or even violent.

- Feminine energy might lead to self-doubt, being too passive, or overreacting.

These traits aren't tied to being a man or a woman. They're just potential pitfalls of each energy. The goal is to find a healthy balance between both energies for our overall wellbeing and happiness.

Here's a simplified way to think about these energies:

Masculine – Fire – Doing energy – Propels us into action

- Build, Fix, Protect

- Strong, Self-Confident

- Logical, Analytical

- Independent, Competitive

Feminine – Water – Being energy – Allows us to feel

- Create, Inspire, Nurture

- Supportive, Compassionate

- Intuitive, Empathetic

- Connected, Receptive

Balance is key. As ultra-independents, we've mastered many masculine traits. Now, it's time to explore and integrate our feminine side.

Take a moment to reflect:

- In your daily life, which masculine and feminine traits do you use most often?

- Do you ever switch between these energies on purpose?

- Which energy feels more natural to you? Which one is more challenging?

Remember, there's no right or wrong answer. It's about understanding yourself better and finding a balance that works for you. By embracing both your masculine and feminine energies, you're not giving up your independence - you're expanding your toolkit for navigating life's challenges.

Personal Experience: The Masculine Mask

I spent years living in my masculine energy, not because I wanted to, but because I thought it was necessary. It was like a suit of armor, protecting me from a world that often felt like a wild and unforgiving jungle. This was my way of surviving, and I'm sure many other fiercely independent women can relate. We put up a tough front, projecting an image of invincibility, because we believe it's what we need to succeed. But the truth is, it takes a heavy toll on us - draining our energy and leaving us exhausted.

For the longest time, I saw femininity as a weakness, a chink in the armor that could be easily exploited. In my mind, being feminine meant being vulnerable, soft, and easily manipulated. And in this dog-eat-dog world? That felt like a recipe for disaster.

Remember all those films and TV shows we grew up watching? The ones where successful career women were always portrayed as cold-hearted bitches? Yeah, those didn't exactly give us the best role models for balancing our feminine and masculine energies. Every TV show seemed to reinforce this belief. My first mentor in the corporate world was a woman who taught me that raising your voice was the key to earning respect. I followed her lead, thinking that instilling fear was the only way to be taken seriously in a man's world.

So, I leaned hard into my masculine energy. I became the doer, the achiever, the one who always had it together. I thought this was the only way to survive, to thrive, to be taken seriously. And you know what? It worked... or so I thought.

After my divorce, I found myself in this weird pattern of choosing emotionally weak men who needed saving. I convinced myself that I was tapping into my feminine energy by fixing their lives. But I wasn't being feminine at all. I was still operating from my masculine side. To these men, I was like the knight in shining armor, the strong one swooping in to save the day.

Looking back, I can see why I couldn't have dated a man who was truly in his positive masculine energy. I would have been fighting tooth and nail to maintain that masculine lead role. It was like I had this need to be the "man" in the relationship, even though deep down, I was craving a strong masculine presence in my life.

I had absolutely no clue how to let someone like that in. I was so used to being the fixer, the doer, the one in control, that the idea of surrendering to someone else's strength was terrifying. My entire self-esteem was wrapped up in what I could do for others. Giving, fixing, saving - that's where I found my worth. It was like I had this invisible scorecard, and the more I could help or "fix" someone, the higher my value.

I surrounded myself with other ultra-independent women who were also living in their masculine energy. We were like a tribe of Amazons, fierce and unyielding. We'd look at more feminine women and, I hate to admit it, but we'd judge them. We saw their softness as weakness, their openness as naivety.

Looking back, I realize how skewed my perception was. I was so engulfed in my masculine energy that I couldn't see the strength in femininity. I couldn't appreciate the power of vulnerability, the courage it takes to be open and receptive in a world that often punishes those traits.

It took me years to realize that true strength isn't about being tough all the time. It's about having the courage to be both strong and soft, to know when to push and when to yield. But man, was that a hard lesson to learn.

Here's the thing: living solely in your masculine energy might help you survive, but it won't help you thrive. It's like trying to write with only your dominant hand – sure, you can do it, but you're missing out on the full range of your capabilities.

So, if you're reading this and thinking, "Oh crap, this sounds just like me," don't worry. Recognizing the pattern is the first step towards change. And let me tell you, embracing your feminine energy alongside your masculine doesn't make you weak – it makes you whole. It's about finding that balance, that sweet spot where you can be both the warrior and the nurturer, both the doer and the receiver.

It's not an easy journey, but it's so worth it. Because when you can dance between your masculine and feminine energies? That's when you truly become unstoppable.

Balancing Masculine and Feminine Energies: Valerie's Journey

Let me introduce you to my client Valerie. She's been on quite a journey these past few years. When we first started working together, Valerie was fresh out of a divorce, trying to navigate the dating world again. Fast forward a bit, and she's found the man of her dreams, gotten married, and they've blended their families - we're talking five kids under one roof!

But Valerie's success wasn't limited to her love life. She also landed her dream job. Sounds perfect, right? Well, not quite. This job has her traveling every month, and it's taking a toll on her relationships at home.

Now, don't get me wrong - Valerie loves her work. But there's tension building at home. Her husband's feeling neglected, the kids are missing her, and Valerie's caught in the middle, trying to balance it all.

During our video calls, I can see the struggle written all over her face. She's torn between her passion for her career and her love for her family. It's that classic ultra-independent woman dilemma - we want it all, we think we can do it all, but sometimes something's got to give.

Identifying the Imbalance

Our first step was to help Valerie recognize her overreliance on masculine energy. We created an "Energy Log" where Valerie tracked her daily activities and the energy she used for each:

Tool: The Energy Log

- Valerie noted her activities throughout the day.

- For each activity, she marked whether she was in masculine energy (doing, achieving) or feminine energy (being, receiving).

- We reviewed the log together, noticing patterns and imbalances.

This exercise was eye-opening for Valerie. She realized that even in situations where feminine energy might be more appropriate - like family dinners or bedtime with the kids - she was still operating in "go mode."

Introducing Feminine Energy

To help Valerie tap into her feminine side, we started with a simple meditation practice:

Tool: Feminine Energy Mini-Meditation

- I guided Valerie through a visualization exercise. In it, she imagines herself sitting by a moonlit river, enveloped in silence. She listens to the gentle flow of water while gazing at the night sky, fully present in the moment.

- We practiced just "being" in the moment, without trying to change or achieve anything.

- Valerie focused on softening and receiving the nurturing energy around her.

At first, Valerie found this challenging. "It feels like I'm wasting time," she admitted. But as we continued the practice, she began to notice subtle shifts in her mood and energy levels.

Practical Applications

Next, we worked on incorporating more feminine energy into Valerie's daily life:

Tool: Feminine Energy Integration Plan

We created a list of simple ways Valerie could practice feminine energy:

- Start the day with gratitude instead of a to-do list.

- Practice active listening without trying to solve problems.

- Ask for help from her partner or kids.

- Spend time in nature weekly.

- Engage in a creative activity for pure enjoyment.

Valerie started small, choosing one item from the list each day. She found asking for help particularly challenging, but also surprisingly rewarding. "When I let my husband take over bedtime routine one night, I realized he had his own special way with the kids. It was beautiful to watch," she shared.

Balancing Work and Home

Valerie's frequent work travel was a major source of stress. We developed strategies to help her maintain connection with her family while honoring her career:

Tool: The Connection-Career Balance Plan

- Quality over quantity: When home, Valerie practiced being fully present.

- Staying connected on the road: We set up regular video calls and surprise notes for her family.

- Embracing vulnerability: Valerie practiced opening up to her partner about her struggles.

This was a turning point for Valerie. By allowing herself to be vulnerable with her partner, she found a deeper level of support she hadn't experienced before.

"I've always been the one to handle everything," Valerie shared during one of our sessions. "It felt strange to let my husband step in and take care of things."

We worked on helping Valerie see that allowing her husband to take a protective role wasn't about surrendering her independence, but about creating a partnership where both could shine in their strengths.

One evening, exhausted from a long business trip, Valerie decided to put our discussions into practice. Instead of pushing through her fatigue to handle family matters, she turned to her husband and said, "I'm really drained. Could you take the lead tonight?"

To her surprise, her husband rose to the occasion beautifully. He managed the kids' bedtime routines, dealt with a minor crisis involving a lost homework assignment, and even prepared a soothing cup of tea for Valerie.

"It was amazing," Valerie reported in our next session. "He wasn't domineering at all. He was just... protective. Caring. It felt like he was creating a safe space for me to just be, without having to do anything. And the kids responded so well to him taking charge."

This experience was transformative for Valerie. She realized that by allowing her husband to step into a protective role, she wasn't diminishing her own strength – she was creating space for a different kind of strength to flourish in their relationship.

"I used to think I had to do it all to be strong," Valerie reflected. "Now I see that true strength is knowing when to lead and when to let others lead. It's about trust and partnership, not control."

This shift in perspective had a ripple effect on their relationship. Valerie's husband felt more valued and engaged in family life, while Valerie found she had more energy for both her work and her family when she allowed herself to lean on her partner's support.

Finding Her Ikigai

To help Valerie find fulfillment in both her career and personal life, we explored the concept of ikigai:

Tool: Ikigai Reflection

I guided Valerie through four key questions:

- What activities make you lose track of time?

- What skills come naturally to you?

- What problems in the world light a fire in your belly?

- How might you turn these passions and skills into a livelihood?

Through this reflection, Valerie realized that her current job, while exciting, wasn't fully aligned with her ikigai. This led to some soul-searching about her long-term career goals.

Cultivating Gratitude

To further nurture Valerie's feminine energy, we introduced a daily gratitude practice:

Tool: The Gratitude Journal

- Every night, Valerie wrote down three things she was grateful for.

- We encouraged her to really feel the gratitude as she wrote.

- During our sessions, we discussed how this practice was impacting her overall outlook.

Over time, Valerie noticed she was finding more joy in small moments and feeling more connected to her family.

The Results

After several months of work, Valerie had made significant progress. She was more comfortable embracing her feminine energy, which paradoxically made her more effective in her masculine-oriented career. Her relationships at home improved as she learned to be more present and vulnerable.

Most importantly, Valerie discovered that balancing her masculine and feminine energies wasn't about changing who she was, but about expanding her range of responses to life's challenges.

"I used to think being feminine meant being weak," Valerie reflected in our final session. "Now I see it as a different kind of strength. I'm still the same driven, successful woman I've always been. But now I have more tools in my toolkit. I can be both the warrior and the nurturer, both the doer and the receiver. And that feels pretty amazing."

Practical Exercises for Balancing Your Energies

Now that we've explored Valerie's journey, let's focus on how you can begin to balance your own masculine and feminine energies. Remember, this isn't about completely changing who you are. It's about expanding your repertoire and giving yourself more options for how to show up in the world.

Your Balancing Act Toolkit

I've put together a toolkit to help you explore and integrate these masculine and feminine energies in your daily life. Think of these exercises as your personal training program for building balance and harmony.

Exercise 1: Practicing Feminine Energy in Daily Life

Incorporate more feminine energy into your daily routine with these simple practices:

- Begin your day with gratitude instead of a to-do list.

- Listen to someone without trying to fix their problem.

- Ask for help (I know it's challenging, but keep trying, it will get easier, I promise).

- Stand in the present moment without planning what's next.

- Trust your intuition.

- Spend time in nature.

- Get creative - try art, journaling, music, or whatever feels good to you.

- Hang out with women who embody their femininity.

- Practice self-love and appreciate your body.

- Embrace the unknown with trust (it's scary, but liberating).

Start small - choose one or two practices to incorporate into your daily routine.

Exercise 2: Balancing Act - Integrating Masculine and Feminine

Try these exercises to find balance:

Masculine Pursuits with a Feminine Twist:

- Try public speaking (masculine) but focus on connecting with your audience (feminine).

- Tackle a challenging project at work (masculine) while nurturing your team's growth (feminine).

Feminine Activities with a Masculine Edge:

- Enjoy a relaxing bath (feminine) while setting intentions for your week (masculine).

- Practice yoga (feminine) with a focus on building strength (masculine).

Mindful Energy Shifts:

- Notice how you show up in different situations. Are you all fire in a moment that needs some water?

- Practice consciously shifting between energies. Lead a meeting with confidence, then listen with empathy.

Exercise 3: Masculine and Feminine Energy Inventory

Grab a journal and for each area of your life, jot down how you express masculine and feminine energies:

- Work/Career

- Relationships (romantic, family, friends)

- Self-care and personal growth

- Hobbies and interests

- Community involvement

For example, in your career, you might write:

Masculine: Setting ambitious goals, leading team meetings

Feminine: Mentoring junior colleagues, trusting my intuition on projects

Exercise 4: Energy Shift Challenge

For one week, choose a daily situation where you'll consciously shift your energy. If you typically approach a task with masculine energy, try leading with feminine energy instead (or vice versa).

Exercise 5: Ikigai Deep Dive

Explore these questions:

- What do you love? What activities make time fly by?

- What are you good at? What skills come naturally to you?

- What does the world need? What problems or challenges call to you?

- What can you be paid for? How might your passions and skills translate into a livelihood?

Look for intersections between these areas to find your potential ikigai.

Exercise 6: Gratitude and Awe Journal

For one week, end each day by writing:

- Three things you're grateful for

- One moment of awe or wonder you experienced that day

Exercise 7: Self-Compassion Check-In

Place a hand on your heart and say to yourself:

"I'm learning and growing. It's okay to be a work in progress. I honor both my masculine and feminine energies."

Reflection:

- How did these practices make you feel?

- How did they impact your interactions with others?

- In which areas of your life do you tend to use more masculine energy?

- Where do you naturally embody more feminine energy?

- Can you identify situations where you might benefit from shifting your energy?

- What changes did you notice in your mood, perspective, or sense of connection to the world around you?

- What felt challenging? What felt surprisingly good?

- Where do you see imbalances in your life? Where might you benefit from tapping into more masculine or feminine energy?

Remember, balance looks different for everyone. Your sweet spot might be 60/40, or 70/30. The key is finding what feels right for you. By practicing these exercises and reflecting on your experiences, you'll start to develop a more intuitive sense of when to employ each energy. This balance will help you navigate life's challenges with greater ease and authenticity.

You've got this. By embracing all aspects of yourself - the doer and the be-er, the fire and the water - you're creating a life that's richer, more fulfilling, and more authentically you.

In our final chapter, we will explore how to incorporate spirituality into our daily lives, using all that we have discovered as a means to achieve deep harmony and connectedness.

Chapter Fifteen

Spirituality – The Unconventional Heroine's Journey

The power of one is magnified through the silent threads of spiritual connection that bind us all.

A Journey's End and Beginning

The sun dips below the horizon, casting a warm glow over the four women standing atop a breezy hill. Sarah, Tamzin, Mia, and Linda are at their own personal thresholds - both literal and figurative. The wind carries the scent of salt and possibility, tousling their hair and clothing as if trying to shed their old selves.

Sarah closes her eyes and tilts her face toward the setting sun before breaking the silence. "Do you remember when we first met?" she asks with a smile tugging at her lips. "We were all so..."

"Closed off," Tamzin finishes, her usual sharp attire replaced by flowing fabric that dances in the wind.

"Exhausted," Mia adds, twisting a wildflower between her fingers absentmindedly.

"Alone," Linda says softly, reaching out to squeeze Mia's shoulder.

They share a knowing glance, each remembering the burdens they once carried - the constant drive, the fear of vulnerability, the exhaustion from always being in control. But here, on this cusp between their past and future, something new stirs within them.

Sarah pulls out a smooth stone from her pocket, inscribed with one word: "Trust." The others follow suit, revealing their own talismans - Tamzin's reads "Surrender," Mia's "Connect," and Linda's "Embrace."

"These stones have been our companions," Sarah says with emotion thick in her voice. "Reminders of the lessons we've learned and the growth we've embraced."

Without a word, they form a circle, holding out their stones in the center. For a moment, they stand there feeling the weight of their journeys in their palms.

Then, as if by an unspoken agreement, they all pull back their arms and toss their stones into the ocean below. Four arcs glimmer in the fading light before vanishing into the waves, taking with them their need for control, their fear of dependence, and their exhaustion from constant self-reliance.

As they step back from the edge, a sense of lightness descends upon the group. The path behind them is littered with remnants of their old beliefs - the fear of vulnerability, the armor of independence, the fatigue of always being on guard. They have faced each of these shadows, not conquering them, but embracing them as part of their journey.

Tamzin is the first to laugh - a rich, full sound that fills the landscape. The others join in, their laughter a celebration of release, joy, and connection.

"Now what?" Mia asks as their laughter fades, her eyes sparkling with endless possibilities.

Linda smiles and reaches out to clasp hands with the others. "Now we start again. Because this journey never truly ends, does it?"

They stand in silence for a moment, hand in hand, feeling the strength of their bond. The fiercely independent women they once were have not disappeared - that strength still exists within them, now balanced with softness and the ability to receive as well as give, to flow instead of constantly pushing.

As the last rays of sunlight paint the sky, Sarah, Tamzin, Mia, and Linda turn away from the cliff's edge. They walk down the hill together toward an uncertain but promising future. Their steps are light and unburdened, perfectly synchronized.

They are whole. They are home. And their adventure is just beginning.

The Heart of the Heroine

Remember that classic story of a hero's journey you've seen in movies and read about in books? Well, guess what - we're living our own version of it, with some unique twists and turns. It all starts when life throws us a curveball - maybe a midlife crisis or a nagging feeling that there's more to life than just self-reliance and success.

This is our call to adventure. It's the universe nudging us, saying, "It's time to break out of your comfort zone!"

But this isn't a leisurely walk through a self-discovery park. It's more like stumbling through a dark forest, facing all the things we've avoided for years. Our fears, wounds, and limiting beliefs all come to light.

However, this is where the real magic happens. It's messy, uncomfortable, and there will be moments when we want to retreat into our old patterns. But as we push through the chaos, we uncover strengths we never knew existed. We become emotional alchemists, turning pain into power and scars into wisdom.

And just when we think we can't take anymore, when it seems easier to give up - that's when the true transformation occurs. We catch a glimpse of our authentic selves - powerful and radiant like a phoenix rising from the ashes of our old lives.

Upon returning to our regular lives, everything looks different. Not because the world has changed, but because we have changed. We have delved deep into ourselves, and there's no turning back after that.

But this journey isn't a one-time deal. It's more like a spiral staircase. We encounter similar themes but from a higher perspective each time. It's an ongoing process of shedding old layers and stepping into new versions of ourselves that are more true and authentic.

Embracing Your Inner World of Imagination

One of the most powerful tools in your spiritual toolkit is something you've had all along: your imagination.

As kids, we were imagination experts. We spent hours playing make-believe, creating wild adventures without worrying if they made sense. But as we got older, people told us to grow up and focus on the "real world" instead.

But what if that message was completely wrong?

Your brain can't tell the difference between what's real and what you imagine. Try this:

Close your eyes and picture a lemon. See its bright yellow skin. Now, imagine cutting it open. Watch the juice drip out. Smell its tangy scent. Think about taking a bite. Is your mouth watering? That's your body reacting to a lemon that's not even there!

Now, imagine you're somewhere peaceful - like a beautiful beach or quiet forest. Use all your senses:

- What do you see?

- What sounds do you hear?

- Can you feel the sun's warmth or a gentle breeze?

As you picture this calm place, notice how your body feels. Your breathing might slow down. Your muscles might relax. This is your own special place to escape when life gets tough.

This isn't just a cool trick. It's a powerful way to beat stress and anxiety. When you're feeling overwhelmed, using your imagination can help you calm down.

Embracing the Divine Feminine

Our spiritual journey invites us to reclaim and embrace the qualities that we have pushed aside in our pursuit of independence. It's about learning to receive and go with the flow, to listen to our gut feelings and honor our need for rest, play, and enjoyment - recognizing these as key ingredients for a fulfilling life.

We've talked about balancing our Masculine and Feminine energies before. Now, let's explore some ways to connect with our softer side. One effective method is through body-focused practices. This involves stepping back from our busy minds - which can be challenging - and tuning into our bodies instead.

To begin, try setting aside a few minutes each day to simply be aware of your breath and body. Pay attention to the feelings in your skin and the gentle rise and fall of your chest as you breathe. It's natural for your thoughts to wander to your never-ending list of tasks. When this happens, gently guide your focus back to your body.

This practice might feel strange at first, but with time, it can help you feel more grounded and in touch with yourself. The key is to approach it with patience and consistency.

With practice, this can help strengthen our inner wisdom - that gut feeling that knows what we need better than our constantly thinking mind. We may become more aware of our body's patterns and better able to tell the difference between our true wants and what society expects of us.

Another way to honor our feminine energy is through ritual and special spaces. Don't worry - this doesn't mean building a temple in your backyard. It can be as simple as lighting a candle and taking deep breaths before starting the day or creating a support group with close friends.

The key is to approach these practices with self-kindness and curiosity. There's no one right way to connect with our feminine energy. Trust yourself, try things out, and find what feels right for you.

Embracing Interconnectedness

As you go deeper into your spiritual journey, you might start to feel more connected to everything around you. It's like suddenly realizing you're not alone, but part of a big, complex world.

We're used to thinking of ourselves as separate from others, responsible only for our own success. The idea that we're actually connected to and need others can feel strange at first.

But as you start to accept this connection, you might feel a big sense of relief. You realize you don't have to handle everything alone. There's a huge support system out there, even when life gets tough.

This doesn't mean giving up your independence. Instead, it's about learning to work with the bigger forces in your life. It's about trusting that the universe is on your side, even when things seem messy or confusing.

One way to cultivate this sense of connection is through a practice called loving-kindness meditation.

Here's how it goes:

Find a comfortable position and close your eyes. Take a few deep breaths to settle in.

Start silently repeating these phrases to yourself:

May I be happy.

May I be healthy.

May I be safe.

May I live with ease.

Really try to feel the intention behind these words. If you notice any resistance (like your inner critic piping up with doubts), just acknowledge it and gently redirect your attention back to the phrases.

After a few minutes, expand your focus to include others. Start with someone you love, then gradually widen the circle to include acquaintances, strangers, and even people you find challenging.

May you be happy.

May you be healthy.

May you be safe.

May you live with ease.

As you practice this, you might notice your sense of separation starting to soften. It's like realizing we're all in this messy, beautiful human experience together.

Another way to tap into interconnectedness is through acts of kindness and generosity - whether it's lending an ear to a friend, volunteering at a local charity, or simply smiling at a stranger. Each small gesture creates ripples that weave a web of connection for us all.

The Ultimate Promise

This is the ultimate promise of the spiritual path: not a life free from challenges, but a life lived in harmony with the greater whole. It's a life where ultra-independence and interdependence aren't mutually exclusive, but two sides of the same coin.

So allow yourself to soften. Open up to the mystery and magic of this journey. Keep putting one foot in front of the other, keep following the whispers of your soul.

And remember, you're not alone in this. You're held in the arms of a universe that supports you, that's conspiring in your favor, that's dancing with you even in the challenging times. Trust in the unfolding, trust in the love that surrounds and sustains you.

Keep shining, keep growing, keep embracing the beautiful complexity of your humanity. You've got this, and the world needs your unique light now more than ever.

A Quick Light Meditation to Close Our Journey

Before we wrap up, let me share with you a quick meditation practice. This is something you can do daily to keep yourself grounded and connected to that beautiful, radiant energy within you.

1. Stand straight up so that your feet are flat on the floor. Close your eyes.

2. Imagine a bright white light coming down from the cosmos, through our planet, through the building, and hovering above your head.

3. Below your feet, visualize roots (like tree roots) that come from inside the depth of the earth, through the soil, through the concrete, right through the building into your feet. These roots have you grounded and held solidly by the earth.

4. Now focus on the light hovering above your head - this is the source, the infinite, the light.

5. Breathe in through your nose for 4 counts, hold for 4, then breathe out through your mouth for 4.

6. As you breathe in, feel the light above your head moving into your head. As you breathe out, let the light move down your face, over your eyes, your nose, your mouth, your chin.

7. Continue this process, moving the light through your entire body - neck, shoulders, arms, hands, chest, heart, belly, groin, thighs, knees, calves, ankles, and toes.

8. Once your whole body is filled with light, breathe in deeply and imagine this light twirling through your body from your toes right up to your head.

9. As you breathe out, let the light from within you shoot up through you like a gush of water. This light comes out the top of your head and falls all around you, covering your skin with this bright light, like a shower of light over your body.

10. See yourself rooted to the earth, protected from below, and rooted to the universe, held from above. See the white bright light within you and the protective light around you.

11. Finish with three more deep breaths - in for 4, hold for 4, out for 4.

Try to do this at least once a day, twice if you can. This light will keep you energetically safe and protected.

We're wrapping up our spiritual journey, but this is really just the start. Take a moment to think about how much you've learned and changed. Look forward to all the good things waiting for you as you keep growing and accepting all parts of yourself - including your strong independent side.

You're doing great! Here's to the next exciting part of your life journey!

Chapter Sixteen

Conclusion – Moving Forward

Wow, what a journey we've been on! We've explored our independence, faced some tough truths, and started to embrace connection. Let's recap:

We've seen how past experiences shaped our go-it-alone attitude, often leaving us exhausted. But we've also celebrated the incredible strength that's gotten us this far. You're a superhero, don't forget it!

We've learned that true strength includes asking for help when needed. At work, we saw how our drive can lead to success but also burnout. In relationships, we've explored how letting our guard down can lead to deeper connections.

Those "soft" qualities we've been ignoring - intuition, emotions, nurturing side - aren't weaknesses. They're superpowers waiting to be used!

This journey is just beginning. There will be days when you slip back into old patterns. When that happens, be kind to yourself. Progress isn't a straight line.

You're not alone. You're part of a tribe of awesome people figuring this out together. Reach out, share your stories, and support each other.

Keep exploring and growing. Stay curious about yourself and others. And be kind to yourself along the way.

Exciting news! If you've enjoyed the exercises in this book, check out the "Healing the Ultra-Independent Heart Workbook". It's packed with more activities to support your growth.

I'd love to hear your feedback about the book. Are there other topics you'd like me to explore in future books? This journey has many layers, so there's more to discover. Reach out and chat with me! Follow me on Facebook, Instagram, and Twitter. Join my Facebook group - Healing the Ultra Independent Heart.

Remember, this is just the start of a new chapter. You get to decide what independence means for you now. How can you keep your strength while also connecting with others?

Thank you for letting me be part of your journey. You're stronger than you know and deserve all the love and connection you want.

Here's to growth, balance, and embracing every part of who you are. May your next chapter be full of meaningful relationships, all while keeping your amazing independent spirit.

Keep shining, you gorgeous ultra-independent goddess!

Gail x

www.gailweiner.com

P.S. If this book inspired you, share it with other independent women in your life. Let's start a revolution of balanced, connected, empowered women. The world won't know what hit it!

About the Author

Gail Weiner is a certified life coach specializing in helping ultra-independent individuals transform their lives by cultivating genuine connections without compromising their inherent strength. With a unique blend of compassionate guidance and practical strategies, Gail empowers her clients to balance self-reliance with meaningful relationships.

Before embracing her true calling as a coach, Gail spent two decades thriving in the fast-paced technology industry. She then successfully launched a tech recruitment business, where she combined her industry expertise with her passion for guiding others toward their ideal paths. During this time, Gail observed a recurring struggle among high-achieving individuals: the challenge of balancing personal success with fulfilling relationships.

Driven by a desire to make a deeper impact, Gail transitioned into life coaching, focusing on women who, like herself, sought to harmonize independence with connection. Drawing from her personal journey of healing and growth, she developed a methodology that addresses the specific needs of ultra-independent individuals. Her approach uncovers generational patterns, establishes healthy boundaries, fosters trust and vulnerability, and empowers women to achieve their dreams.

Gail's debut book, *Healing the Ultra-Independent Heart*, and its accompanying workbook, distill her expertise into a comprehensive guide for those seeking balanced, fulfilling lives. Through her writing, coaching, and speaking engagements, Gail continues to inspire and guide individuals on their journey to authentic, connected living. Her work is a testament to the power of embracing one's true calling and the transformative potential of balancing independence with meaningful connection.